THE NATIONAL
MUSEUM OF
HEALTH AND
MEDICINE CHICAGO

19'th Annual Tcl Association
Tcl/Tk Conference
Proceedings
Chicago, IL
November 14-16, 2012

TclA
Publications

TCL Association Publications

Proceedings of the 19'th Annual Tcl/Tk Conference
ISBN: 978-0-578-11807-9

Special thanks to Dawson Cowals for designing
the Tcl Association logo.
For graphic design or web development consult-
ing please visit him on the web at
http://www.dawsoncowals.com/

Table Of Contents

Tcl 2012
Chicago, IL
November 14-16, 2012

Session 1
November 14, 10:45-12:15

Bringing Context to the Internet of Things

Dr. Emmanuel Frécon

This paper is dedicated to my newly become wife

Abstract—**The context manager is aimed at being the hub of the house, a place where all sensors report (directly or indirectly) their data, sometimes in aggregated form, but also where all applications will search for information relevant to them, i.e. sensor values, location or information about their surroundings. The context is instantiated from a dynamic model to fit the needs of a variety of scenarios and settings. The manager provides an easy-to-use Web API and integrates external cloud services relevant for applications running in the house.**

Index Terms—**IoT, Tcl, REST, JSON, Web, Integration, Web Services, Sensors, Actuators, Middleware, Energy, Smart Homes**

I. Introduction

THE Internet of Things promises a near future where domestic and work environments, but also cities and factories, are augmented with sensors and actuators that all are Internet entities. The deployment of IPv6 is key to this evolution by enabling each sensor or actuator to be accessed from any Internet enabled application or user, thus from almost anywhere. The Internet of Things is often seen as the catalyst of more intelligent environments, where applications will use Things to perform actions and sense on our behalf, with little human intervention.

As the number of connected Things will grow, making sense of what is accessible and can be done and how they relate to one another will be harder and harder. For taking good and qualified decisions, applications will not only need to know how to access the sensors and actuators, but also where

Emmanuel Frécon is with the Interactive Collaborative Environments Laboratory, Swedish Institute of Computer Science, Box 1263, SE-16429 Kista, Sweden, e-mail: emmanuel@sics.se.

these are located, the people in their vicinity, their immediate neighbouring Things, etc. The context manager is a modular Tcl[1] web service that attempts to provide this contextual information to applications, i.e. the extra logical layer empowering applications with the overlaying of dynamic sensor data on top of locational data of more static nature. While the context manager primarily targets home environments, it can also be used in other environments. The context manager relies on simple PubSub[2] and pull mechanisms to account for the low resources available on sensors. It also offers a streaming interface based on WebSockets for push and pull of sensor and actuator data.

II. Related Work

There starts to exist a number of cloud-based services that target the IoT (Internet of Things) and provide APIs to store and later retrieve data that has been sent for storage into the cloud. Probably the most well-known of these services is COSM[1] (formerly known as pachube). But there are a number of other services such as sen.se[2], nimbits[3] or thingspeak[4] to mention a few. Common to all those services is a web-based API that is easily integrated directly from sensor platforms, providing tiny (connected) sensors or gateways off-site storage. The same API can be used to retrieve data from

[1]Cosm is available at https://www.cosm.com/ and is open for new account registration.

[2]Sen.se is available at http://open.sen.se/ and is open for beta testing by the way of invitations only.

[3]Nimbits is available at http://www.nimbits.com/ and is open for new account registration. Nimbits also touts private cloud solutions by allowing the integration of the nimbits solution within existing architectures.

[4]Thingspeak is available at https://www.thingspeak.com/ and is open for new account registration

the web services, thus opening up for data-mining activities if ever necessary. Common to those APIs is the use of REST[3] and JSON[4] for retrieving and posting data from and to the cloud. This is to ease integration from low-power consumer-oriented hardware platforms such as arduino[5] or gadgeteer[6].

In addition to providing an "infinite" data storage for sensors and actuators, the power of these services lies in the community of people around them and the ability to integrate values from several sources to reason in improved and more sensible ways. In short, these services provide a whole ecosystem of devices, applications and people, by being able to pinpoint sensors using location services and providing ways to get notified whenever their value change. From the point of view of a house and household, sen.se seeks to take a step further by allowing users to build user interfaces to control their houses. Sen.se provides ways for its users to visually create applications by connecting sensors to web-side logic boxes and finally present the resulting "computation" through its dashboard, a web-based UI combining output of values with input of commands to be utterly received by actuators.

However, these services fail to provide more information about the context within which all these sensors and actuators are being placed, especially when it comes to smaller scale installations such as a house or a building. In order to be able to make energy-smart decisions, leading to smart actuation of the devices that are accessible to them, applications need to know about inhabitants, relative locations of sensors, external conditions, etc. So far, the merging of the Semantic Web[7] with sensor networks, also known as the Sensor Web or the Sensor Internet [8][9][10][11] has focused on the creation of specifications for different functionalities related to the management of sensor-based data (observations, measurements, sensor network descriptions, transducers, data streaming, etc.), and for the different types of services that may handle these data sources (planning, alert, observation and measurement collection and management, etc.). The

cost of providing network abstraction and ontologies often comes with increased complexity. So while these middlewares effectively provides ways to reason about devices and actuators at a high level, they seldom solve the problem of providing the general context while still lowering the threshold for regular users.

III. GOALS

The context manager is aimed at being the nav of the house, i.e. the place where all relevant sensors report (directly or indirectly) their data, sometimes in aggregated form, but also where all applications will dig for information that is relevant to them, i.e. both values from some sensors, but also their location or information about their surroundings. Being such a nav, the context manager is designed to be placed and hosted in a home gateway, i.e. a "number crunching" appliance that provides computing power and intelligence at a lower price in a central place[5]. In this context, houses are taken in their larger forms and can be entire buildings if necessary, and the design should open up for federations of context managers to adapt to the needs and privacy concerns of both building owners and flat owners (or inhabitants).

The main goal of the context manager is to provide dynamic ways to model the context, e.g. a house and all its online devices, be them sensors or actuators. The dynamism of the context is essential at different levels: first it is important to be able to host new devices as they are installed in the house, secondly it is important to be able to model the context in various ways because all houses are far from being the same and because there might be cultural differences between location that have an impact on the context itself. Consequently, the context manager takes an object-oriented approach, where the possible content of the context, i.e. the objects themselves is driven and controlled by a simple schema, i.e. a model of what objects can be made available in the context, but also a model

---

[5]The current implementation of the context manager has been verified to be fully functional on the open source Beagle-Board xM, an ARM A8 development board.

of their relations. The use of schemas could introduce complexity to the conceptual approach, so the context manager features a simplified schema with few rules and in a human-readable format. Several schemas can be aggregated, allowing for experts to provide base schemas, perhaps somewhat more complex in their form while still providing power to the end users and the inhabitants, so as to adapt to the specific needs of a household, a building or a custom-made online sensor.

The context manager seeks to provide an open API that follows the current trends within Web-based services and development. Web asynchronous communication is slowly moving from SOAP[12] and XML[13] standards into REST and JSON for a number of reasons. One of the advantages of these new standards are their ease of reading, i.e. core communication can be tested directly in the web browser, and the results from a query are easily read in a textual format that is much more compact than XML. It is out of the scope of this document to advocate for either one or the other standard, but since the context manager aims at providing an easy interface to application programmers, REST/JSON are more suitable to the task. Apart from allowing programmers to test queries against an existing instance, both the format of the queries and of the result are in general less cumbersome to parse, thus easily integrated into existing code and onto low-power platforms such as mobile phones or even sensor platforms.

IV. DESIGN

A. Schema and Model

In order to cope with different sorts of environments and to account for the cultural differences between housings in various regions of the world, the context manager is based on a dynamic schema that directs the content of the objects that will be instantiated to describe a house or any other environment. The schema can include remote (web) schemas, thus providing ways for experts and/or interested users to collaborate, but also providing for the inclusion of new classes of objects that will support newly created sensors. In order to

easily be accessible to technically inclined users, the schema supports few paradigms: single inheritance, a few base types (`Boolean`, `Integer`, `Float`, `String`, `Timestamp`[14] and arrays) and constraints. Constraints describe rules to which field values should comply to, providing minimum and maximum bounds or constraining only a few possible values. Constraints offer a way to model physical units and laws: for example, temperature can be expressed in Celsius and is always greater than -274.15. The syntax for the schema minimises idioms and is designed to be human-readable with lesser effort.

Objects modeling the context are instantiated from the schema, and sensors and/or external services will update the fields of these objects as new values are measured, made available or acquired. Initial instantiation will provide decent default values for all fields and subsequent updates will always be checked against the possible constraints that direct the content of one or several fields. The context manager provides a number of techniques for remote services to be notified when objects and their contained fields are modified as time passes.

B. Data Flow and Storage

The context manager reads its schema (and included schemas) during initialisation, subsequently reading a file describing the initial context. Typically, the initial context will be composed of more or less transient information such as the rooms composing a house together with their interconnections, but also an initial instantiation of the objects that will be involved in the dynamic representation of devices, sensors, actuators and inhabitants, together with their spatial relations. Modification of fields in objects, and queries for the inter-relationships is supported by a REST/JSON inspired API.

The API supports (basic) authentication and HTTPS[15] encryption if necessary, because of their widespread use and their ability to scale down to the few resources available on sensors. As times goes by, all values set are automatically mirrored to a noSQL database (cluster) implemented on top of REDIS[16]. The API supports access to historical data. It also enables setting values in the future, thus supporting prediction. Whenever the scheduled time is reached, a value will automatically be set to the one that had been set in the future. The API also permits setting values in the past for the automated storage of historical data. So-called triggers implement a PubSub mechanism, allowing remote Web services, applications and sensors to be notified whenever value(s) in objects change upon given conditions. Finally, WebSockets[17] can be kept opened against particular objects, offering both a way to stream updates from the object as time passes, but also to update its fields whenever needed.

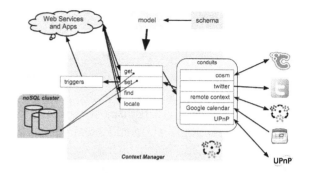

Figure 1.   The API of the context manager provides REST/JSON entry points both to query the state of the context, but also to modify it. In addition, it supports external known and generic Web Services, while being able to predict and automatically store historical data through a connected noSQL database.

C. Extensibility through Conduits

The context manager is extensible through the concept of "conduits". Conduits are logical entities connected to external web services that will direct data into or from the context depending on a number of conditions. Typically, conduits will perform some transformation on the data to or from the external web service, while also retaining data that is specific to the remote service, e.g. login credentials, authorisation details, session information, etc. At present, there are conduits for Twitter, for import and export of data to the COSM cloud service, to remote context managers, to nearby UPnP objects and services and for the control of objects' values according to Google calendar bookings. Conduits are loaded as a set of plugins during the initialisation phase, they access the context manager through its modular internal API.

V. IMPLEMENTATION

A. Functionality

The context manager roughly provides the following set of functionality:

- It takes a schema and a model to provide a logical context of a building. This context can be accessed and modified using REST/JSON calls for maximised flexibility and integration. This means that most operations to and from

the context can actually be made (tested?) from the comfort of any Web browser[6].

- The context manager provides a number of ground operations to:
  - Get the content of whole or part of the context, including the values of the fields of the instantiated objects and including values from the past, whenever they are accessible.
  - Modify values of objects that already are instantiated, which will be an operation that is often used when the value of a sensor changes.
  - Provides means to search for objects by the content of their field, the name of their class, etc.
  - Provides means to understand arrays as a technique to organise (part of) the model in a hierarchy and to find specific objects within such a hierarchy.
  - Provides means to trigger external web services whenever (part of) an object has changed, i.e. to mediate the content of the object to remote Web Services. Triggers offer enough flexibility so as to be able to:

[6]There are several JSON formatting extensions for most of the Web browsers. Such an extension will be necessary since the context manager minimises output by removing all unnecessary indentation or line breaks.

* Restrict which field of the object are under watch and how to mediate their value to the remote service, i.e. as part of the URL, in the body of the posted data, etc.
* Specify in details the headers, the MIME type and the method of the HTTP request (GET, POST, PUT, DELETE).
* Control the maximum frequency of this mediation to avoid flooding the network.
* Mediate only under certain conditions, expressed as a mathematical expression involving any of the fields of the object (based on the Tcl `expr` command).
* Control if mediation should happen every time the value is updated, or only if it has changed since last time (the default).

– Provides means to stream the flow of changes to remote clients via WebSockets, expressed as JSON representations of the object. This interface provides approximately the same level of control as the triggers described above[7]. WebSockets have two advantages:

* They easily pass through firewalls and multi-level NAT hierarchies, thus making sure that even clients at the edges of the network can be notified of changes.
* Once the connection has been established, packets containing object data are kept to a minimal (with almost no additional overhead or verbose header), which makes them suitable for transmission across WSN (wireless sensor networks).

– Automatically saves versions of objects to a database for later retrieval. Given the unstructured nature of the context, noSQL databases are a perfect match, especially since they form the base of a number of data-mining techniques.

• The context manager offers a pluggable architecture through the concept of "conduits", i.e. logical entities connected to external web services that will direct data to or from the model depending on a number of conditions. Typically, conduits will perform some transformation on the data to or from the external web service, while also retaining data that is specific to the remote service, e.g. login credentials, authorisation details, session information, etc. There are a number of conduits already available:

– The COSM conduit is able to pull and push data from the COSM Cloud service. The conduit supports both the access of non-public feeds via an API key and to public feeds, polling their content at the necessary frequency whenever needed. Data can be transformed on the way to and from the feeds, matching *feed* names against *fields* names in the context manager, but also performing any mathematical operation supported by the `expr` command at copy time.

– The remote context conduit is able to pull and push data from remote context managers, using triggers at the remote managers to get notified of changes. The conduit can be forced to poll for data instead to ease firewall and NAT traversal. As for the COSM conduit, data can be transformed on the way to and from the remote context. Being able to incorporate (parts of) remote context into a local context opens up for the creation of federations of context, and the ability to (re)use the sensors of your neighbours when taking decisions.

– The local context conduit is a simplification of the remote conduit that only acts between local objects. It allows for the transfer (and transformation) of fields

---

[7]All control that is only relevant to how the HTTP request to the external Web service should be made are left aside since this is not relevant in the case of WebSockets, i.e. in a framework that keeps the connection opened at all time.

values between different objects of the context, whenever some conditions are met.

- The Google calendar conduit binds the events of a given calendar to a `Boolean` that will turn `on` when there is a booking in the calendar, and `off` when there is no booking. Combined to local conduits and actuation (see section VII-B2), this can be used to specify when some devices should be turned on or off.

- The UPnP[18] conduit is able to pull and push data from remote UPnP services. The conduit is built on top of an SSDP discovery mechanism, thus being able to bind objects of the context manager to a service that has a given (discovered) name, or to a service that is at a given known location. While the conduit has been designed to bridge the context manager to objects within the LinkSmart middleware[11], it makes a number of assumptions to be able to be used in more generic cases. Similarly to the other conduits, the UPnP conduit is able to push and pull data to and from the known state variable of a UPnP server. For this to work in a generic way, the conduit assumes that the service has methods which name contains the name of the state variable and that contain the keywords "get" or "set" to get or set the content of the variable.

B. Security Mechanisms

There are two intertwined security mechanisms that will control the access to the context manager. First of all, the context manager is able to run on top of HTTPS[15] thus providing encryption of both requests and their results, so as to avoid eavesdropping from external parties. HTTPS was chosen because it is a well-established protocol that is widely supported across languages and platforms. The context manager supports both self-signed and authorised certificates.

Secondly, all web accesses can be controlled by a user name and password that will be mediated to the context manager using Basic Authentication[19]. Control should occur at the (virtual) directory level so as to provide for finer grained access restrictions if necessary. The goal is to refrain some users from, for example, setting the values of some objects of the context. Again, basic authentication was chosen because it is widely supported across languages and platforms. Basic Authentication sends the password from the client to the server unencrypted, however it should be used in conjunction with HTTPS.

There might be cases where HTTPS encryption is too heavy for the client platform in terms of computing resources, for example if sensors send directly their data to the context and/or need to reason about other sensors in their vicinity to take decisions. For those cases, the context manager is able to provide regular HTTP access. This HTTP access should be secured by a set of firewalling rules that will prevent access to the context manager from any remote client except the ones that need to access the manager for the reasons detailed above. Since these cases are most likely to occur within home networks and since most current home installations and Internet accesses are based on NAT techniques, the security risks introduced by unencrypted access in those cases are deemed to be low. In those cases, wires or proximity ensures physical security. This security relies however on proper configuration of the Internet access and the different firewalls involved.

C. Startup and Initialisation

On startup, the context manager will perform the following operations in sequence:

1) The context manager will start a web server with the proper credentials (see V-B) and proper encryption settings. Alternatively, the context manager can be embedded in an existing server framework if more suitable.

2) The web server will expose the schema and model that will define the context of the building or the house that the manager is controlling and modeling.

3) It will read the schema (see VI-A) that will describe what classes of objects are allowed

to appear in the context. This includes possible access to remote schemas that might be included from the main schema. Reading of the main schema might be through accessing the internal web service if necessary[8].

4) It will then read the model (see VI-B) that describes the particular building that it is modeling and controlling. All constraints implied by the schema that has just been read will be applied as the model is being read.

5) All objects instantiated as part of the model are bound to the noSQL engine so that further write operations will automatically lead to new versions of the object being stored and so that later get operations will be able to get older data, whenever possible.

6) It will initialise all conduits that are accessible to this context manager. Conduits are conceptually separated from the remaining of the code and are plugins communicating with the remaining of the context manager through a tiny and well-defined (internal) API.

7) It will read an initial "pairing" state (see VI-C) that is used to initialise a number of conduits and to bind a number of objects to remote services. Pairing is explained later and mostly a helper functionality that aims at reinitialising the context manager every time that it starts and reaching a similar functioning state.

VI. FILE INTERFACES

Instead of providing an entire specification of the file formats that are understood by the context manager, this section focuses on providing real-life (shortened) examples. These examples are annotated and explained, bringing further insights to the internal of the context manager and all the facilities that it offers.

---

[8]Actually, reading the main schema via the web is encouraged since this will enforce UUIDs that remain constant over time and are bound to the specific installation. Preferably, a hostname will be involved in the main URL to bind the instantiated objects, classes and their UUIDs to a specific and logical place.

A. Schema

As highlighted before, the context manager provides techniques to specify the schema that will be used to describe the context itself. A key requirement to the provision of this schema is that it should be easily approachable not only by IT specialists, but also by less-knowledgeable people. To this end the schema brings in object-orientation concepts but simplifies them to their outermost. For example, it provides simple inheritance and mixes both object field specifications and inheritance[9]. The schema does not provide concepts such as private variables or similar, once again for the sake of simplification.

Below is a cut-down example of a schema, providing a flavour of how a schema looks and feels like. Roughly, this example schema divides the space into a number of possible floors and rooms within a building, and enables each part of the space to carry a number of devices (inhabitants are left aside on purpose). The example sports a single type of device, namely a thermometer, which demonstrates the (definition and) use of constraints to provide for a richer expression of units and properties of the physical world. The constraint defines temperature (in Celsius) as a floating point value that always is above the 0K.

```
Space {
  name String
  contains Space[]
  devices Device[]
  Outside {
  }
  Building {
    address Address
    pos Coordinate
  }
  Apartment {
    number Integer
  }
  Floor {
    above Floor
    below Floor
  }
  Room {
```

---

[9]While mixing class hierarchy and description in the same flow might surprise, this solution was chosen for the sake of simplicity. It has the advantage of presenting all data relevant to a given schema at a glance.

```
      Kitchen {
      }
      Bedroom {
      }
      Office {
      }
      Bathroom {
      }
   }
}
Address {
   street String
   streetNumber Integer
   areaCode Integer
   city String
   country String
}
Coordinate {
   latitude Float
   longitude Float
}
Temperature:Float {
   intervals {[-273.15,[}
   unit "celsius"
}
Device {
   name String
   SensorDevice {
      Weather {
         Thermometer {

            value Temperature
         }
      }
   }
}
```

To simplify the approach by non-technical experts, no forward declaration of classes or constraints is necessary. All new "types" that are discovered will be understood as (empty) classes as a start and converted when their real definition occurs. While this has the drawback of more complicated parsing and the possibility of duplicates or of unknown state — what to do when a class with a given name is then specified as a constraint under the same name — these problems are considered minor compared to the necessity to forward declare classes or constraints before being able to use them.

B. Model

The schema only specifies and constraints the types of the objects that should be placed in a model. While the schema is essential to the context manager since it provides guidelines to what can be instantiated within the model, achieving a conceptual model of a home and all its online devices is the ultimate goal of the context manager. To this end, the context manager provides a file format that is easily approachable, allowing people to quickly model their own house. At later stages, and depending on the success of the approach, graphical tools would certainly provide help in specifying the final model, perhaps based on existing drawings (blueprints or CAD).

Below is an extract of a model, based on the example schema above. The purpose of this example is to set the scene and provide a flavour for how model files could look like. Complete models tend to be more extensive, so the example below is not complete.

```
Outside pHataren1 {
   name "PositivHataren1"
   contains {myHouse}
   devices {
      outsideTemp
   }
}
Address aSoderman10 {
   street "August Södermansväg"
   streetNumber 10
   areaCode 12938
   city "Hägersten"
   country "Sweden"
}
# Approximate center of our lot.
Coordinate myPosition {
   latitude 59.299428
   longitude 17.970209
}
# The house contains three floors,
# which will contain the rooms.
Building myHouse {
   name "House Frecon-Waller"
   address aSoderman10
   pos myPosition
   contains {
      ground cellar top
   }
}
```

```
# The different floors in the house,
# here only one for the sake of
# concision.
Floor ground {
  name "Ground Floor"
  contains {
      hall kitchen diningRoom
      livingRoom bath vilma
  }
  above cellar
  below top
}
#######
# Devices
Thermometer outsideTemp {
  name "Temp. sensor outside"
}
```

The model uses the schema to control the content of objects that are created within the model. Every instance of a class is referenced using an identifier. Using techniques similar to those used for the schema, objects can be referenced before they are actually used, but the model provides enough feedback whenever the data that is specified does not correspond to the schema that controls what can be specified.

In the resulting model, both instantiated objects within the model and classes are identified by a UUID[20]. The UUID is of type 3 or 5 and built using a concatenation of the URL to the model (or to the schema), the class name and (when relevant) the reference to the object. This ensures that, even upon restarts, objects and classes will keep their UUIDs as long as the file structure, content and location has not changed.

C. Pairing

In order to be able to restart from a similar state at all times, the context manager is able to read from a pairing configuration file once the schema and the model have been read. The purpose of this file is to establish all the necessary conduit connections to well-known services. Pairing is made at the conduit level, thus at the REST/JSON level. In other words, when initialising the pairing, the context manager behaves as if it was an external client to itself. This is to be able to support new

conduits in the future and to fail nicely if some conduit initialisation did not succeed properly.

Below is an annotated example file showing how pairing can be initialised at start, the syntax provides some visual markup to highlight the source and destination objects and uses a number of heuristics to detect which conduit to use for data migration. An integer is understood as a COSM feed, a UUID as an object from the local context manager, a URL ending with a UUID as an object in a remote context manager, a URN starting with `gcal:` as a Google calendar and a URN starting with `UPnP:` as a UPnP service. The "arrow" of the markup can specify and/or force polling frequency and indentation is used to further specify how the value of fields are carried to the remote entity.

```
# Map my heat pump to the COSM feed with
# identifier 53880. Non-matching
# fields/datastream names will be ignored.
# API key is picked up from the configuration
# of the context manager.
55851044-b290-56a5-3c88-d64ffbfa75e9 -> 53880
# Another COSM mapping, making sure the COSM
# datastream "inside" is mapped to 4 times the
# value of the field "value" in the context
# object,
20ecdbe4-8459-5636-6146-71c618badc71 -> 53882
    %inside% = 4.0*%value%
# Reverse COSM mapping, datastream called "2"
# in feed 55180 at COSM is brought the field
# "value" in the context object.
55180 --> 929494fb-84e1-50cb-beea-c04aecda088a
    %value% = %2%
# Pick up the weather station of somebody else,
# do some field names / datastream mappings and
# force polling to occur every 180 seconds.
45036 -180-> 684c4e19-c4ed-5861-f127-59109a41bb56

    %temperature% = %OutsideTemprature%
    %pressure% = %ABSPressure%
    %humidity% = %OutsideHumidity%
    %rain% = %Rain%
    %windDirection% = %WindDir%
    %windSpeed% = %WindSpeed%
# Send status of context object to the UPnP
# service named "Dev"
5d9a66e5-9738-598c-d0b0-e707eb0e2a36 -> UPnP:Dev
```

VII. APPLICATIONS AND EXAMPLES

This work has been carried out within the framework of a European project looking into energy optimisation. The project uses traditional home automation in order to attain energy savings while still offering the same level of comfort. The project also seeks to offer "soft" actuation mechanisms, i.e. providing enough (summarised) information about some of the decisions taken by devices in the home to let inhabitants take the final necessary steps. Ambient displays are used to carry out this type of information in a form that is aesthetically acceptable. A number of prototype pilot houses have been equipped with sensors and actuators of various forms in order to gather data for future data-mining activities, but also to experiment with how smart actuation can turn into energy savings or reduction of CO_2 emissions. This section describes one of these prototype installations, located in the outskirts of Stockholm. There are several other installations, featuring a slightly different feature set of software and hardware so as to adapt to the particularities of these households: type of heating, electricity meter, etc.

A. Heating and (Inner) Climate

1) Heat Pump Analysis (and Control): Live status from a heat pump (IVT Greenline HT+) is picked up via its service serial interface using software from a small Swedish company called Husdata[10]. This is connected to a PC running Windows sitting on top of the pipe system in the direct vicinity of the heat pump. The default settings within StatLink, the software provided by Husdata as part of their offering have been slightly modify to increase the number of sensors being read and to regularly dump sensor data to a particular location on the PC, a location that is served by a tiny web server[11]. Raw dump data is (remotely) polled by a Tcl script at regular intervals and pushed to the context manager after naming transformations. Within the context manager, a conduit forwards

acquired data to two COSM feeds[12].

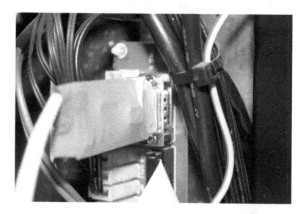

Figure 2.   Husdata provides a hardware module to connect to the service serial interface of the heat pump, together with Windows software for analysing the decisions taken by the pump over time.

Figure 3.   A Windows PC collects data from the heat pump, it is placed on top of a number of copper pipes in direct connection to the pump. The module with an antenna is the root node of the WSN network that collects temperature and main electricity data (see sections VII-A2 and VII-B1).

The current solution only provides gathering of heat pump sensor data. This has been immensely valuable since we can now perform long-term analysis of the behaviour of the heat pump using data-mining techniques, so as to be able to detect with

---

[10]Husdata http://www.husdata.se/ offers a number of hardware modules to connect a computer to a range of heat pump commonly found in Sweden, from several manufacturers.

[11]The current installation relies on mongoose, available at https://github.com/valenok/mongoose.

[12]Converted pump data is pushed to https://cosm.com/feeds/ 53880, temperature is pushed to one of the datastreams of https://cosm.com/feeds/53882, additionally raw data, as taken directly from the husdata software is pushed to https://cosm. com/feeds/52002. This is being used mainly for debugging purposes and for detecting possible failures in the context manager and in the surveillance PC network connection.

this given household will need warm water. It opens up for predicting when it will use warm water in the future, so as to shutdown warm water production during peak hours and start again at off-hours, before warm water is needed again. However, taking these last steps implies being able to control the internal logic of the heat pump, using the serial protocol described at http://rago600.sourceforge.net/.

2) Inner Temperature: A TinyNode[21] board running Contiki[22] and carrying a temperature sensor is hidden behind a photo frame. Measurements are sent along a mesh network at regular intervals, captured via the pump computer and sent on via UDP to a Tcl script. The script automatically pushes data into an object of the context manager, and further to COSM[13] via a conduit.

Figure 4. The TinyNode measuring temperature hides itself behind a photo frame in the living room, so as to break the aesthetics as little as possible. It has been slightly pushed aside for the sake of documentation and picture taking.

This particular heat pump installation only contains an outside temperature sensor, with which all decisions are taken when it comes to heating. The pump is able to host an inner temperature sensor (cabled) to take better decisions about when

[13]Temperature is pushed to one of the feeds https://cosm.com/feeds/53882 that already is used to publish the outside temperature acquired via the heat pump, though to another datastream.

and when not to generate heat. Combined with the planned implementation of serial connection and control of the pump, the provision of a wireless inner sensor could provide for better inner climate without the wiring that is required by regular installations.

3) Weather: A specially written Tcl script can be used to update (in the future) an object of the context manager to reflect the weather forecast for a given location. The script uses the REST/JSON API from the Weather Underground[14] to access an hourly forecast for the coming 10 days. As updates are made in the future for those specific times, they are automatically stored in the noSQL cluster and set back as the "current" value as time passes. The script can be run once in a while or continuously. It will thus keep updating the object with an up-to-date weather forecast, allowing other applications using the context manager to reason about the current and future weather situation. For example, an application that would control heating could make the decision to accept temporary temperature drops if the outside temperature is only going to decrease for a few hours/days. The object that the script sends its data share the same model as a weather station, thus implementing a virtual private weather station in combination with the script.

B. Electricity and Energy Consumption

1) Total Measurement: The past decade has seen the progressive replacement of all electricity meters in Sweden in favours of so-called smart meters. These meters are able to report the hourly electricity consumption to the utility company as time passes, so as to bed for refined billing and better dimensioning of the grid. Pulses from the electricity meter are captured by another TinyNode sensor running Contiki, manufactured by CRL Sweden. Data is pushed out of the sensor network to the same Tcl

[14]Documentation for the API is available at http://www.wunderground.com/weather/api/. There are numerous other services offering the same type of data, Weather Underground was chosen because of its ability to chunk several questions into one request, but also because it is also uses ideas from the Internet of Things: forecast are improved using the data from private weather stations, whenever possible.

bridge as in section VII-A2. The bridge forwards to another object of the context manager, and thus automatically to COSM[15]. This publishes an history of the instantaneous power used by the household over time. As electricity is one of these hidden cost that is seldom understood, an ambient display is at the planning stage; a display that will both visualise how much electricity has been used so far, but also provides feedback to the instantaneous variations, thus to power, required by new devices being switched on (or off).

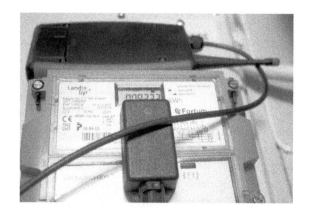

Figure 5. All electricity meters installed in Sweden host a LED (IR or visible) that flashes a number of time for each number of Watts used. The pulse metering node, sitting on top of the meter itself, continuously count these pulses and reports the total count for the latest period via the WSN network.

2) Measurement and Control at the Device Level: PlugWise are smart plugs manufactured by a Dutch company. They form a ZigBee mesh radio network, allowing access and control from a computer to which a specific USB key is connected. They offer three key features.

1) They host a relay, meaning that they are able to turn on or off all the devices connected to the plug and this from a distance. The state of the physical relay can be queried at any time.

2) They measure the instantaneous power being used by all devices connected to the plug, a value that can be requested from a distance.

---

[15]The COSM feed https://cosm.com/feeds/60040 is updated at two minutes interval with the current power consumption of the whole house

---

3) They keep an hourly log of the electricity consumption related to the plug. As this log is kept in memory in the plug itself, historical data for the plug can be accessed from a distance at later time if necessary. The log rotates with time but keeps a few days worth of hourly data.

A Tcl script couples one or several objects from the context manager to as many smart plugs as there are objects. At the core of the Tcl bridge is a wrapper library around the command line interface of one[23] of the open source libraries created to access the PlugWise hardware and network. The bridging script connects to object representations of the plugs in the context manager using the WebSocket API[16] and pushes all information, including relay state and historical data, gathered from the plug. The state of the relay is represented by a `Boolean` and turning the field on and off in the context manager will be propagated to the physical plug, allowing to turn on and off connected electrical devices.

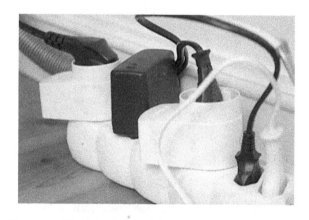

Figure 6. The form factor of the smart plugs from PlugWise (white plugs on the picture) make them easy to install across the house in order to measure the consumption of particular devices, but also to automatically turn on and off (sets of) devices based on heuristic such as the time of the day, the day of the week, or more advanced schemes in response to Demand/Response requirements from the grid.

---

[16]In order to be able to resist to network equipment that restrict the use of WebSockets, the plugwise bridge is also able to poll at regular intervals for the desired state of the physical relay.

3) Spot Prices: The Swedish electricity market has been deregulated for a number of years and prices vary on an hourly basis, dividing Sweden in four different geographical regions. Nord Pool Spot runs the power market in Sweden and offers day-ahead prices to its customers. A Tcl script continuously acquire the prices[17] for all regions and updates one or several objects of the context to reflect the current price at that location.

C. Ambient Interfaces

An off-the-shelf multi-coloured lamp is put under the control of a REST-based server written in Tcl. Controlling of the lamp is via the IR from Dangerous Prototypes[18]. At present and for time reason, the solution only works on Windows, on top of WinLIRC. The lamp can take a wide number of colours and the REST interface accepts any RGB codes, approximating to the closest available colour on the lamp.

Figure 7.   The design of the lamp makes it an acceptable display for home "events" in a number of cases.

A second Tcl REST server offers a Web interface to "tune" the lamp to various data sources present in the context manager. The user interface is kept

---

to a bare minimum, but is easily accessible from both computers and mobile devices, which is the expected future scenario. Using colours, the lamp can visualise the live status of the heat pump (from green when not working to purple when using external heat), the temperature inside or outside, the price of the electricity on Spot, etc.

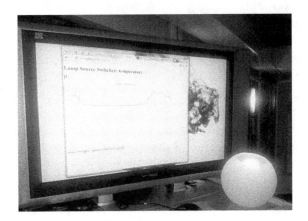

Figure 8.   In the figure above, the lamp is tuned to the outside temperature and the user interface is shown on nearby TV for demo purposes. The UI uses the COSM connection to display relevant historical graphs.

VIII. CONCLUSIONS AND FUTURE WORK

This paper has presented the context manager, a central hub designed both to provide contextual data to IoT applications and a storage for historical, present and future sensor and actuator data. The context manager is designed to lower the learning curve, letting less technically inclined people model and reason about their smart homes. Concepts such as pairing, conduits and triggers lean themselves easily to be controlled and specified via user interfaces rather than via the file formats that have been summarised in this document. As such, these concepts already contain parts of the logic that would control the flow of data between different objects, combined to both actuation and visualisation through external services. Possible extensions would consist in looking into visual programming efforts such as App Inventor[24] and ways to incorporate some of these ideas into the IoT domain. Already, colleagues have started to work on the

---

[17]Prices are scraped from http://www.nordpoolspot.com/ for historical reasons.

[18]The IR toy is a set of open source hardware and software available at http://dangerousprototypes.com/docs/USB_IR_Toy_v2 to record and (re)play the IR codes of most infrared-based remote controls.

building blocks of an "appification" of the home, i.e. the installations of "apps" that can control parts of your homes to attain some energy savings, while providing a (mobile) user interface to input settings and refine controlling. For this "appification" to take place, applications will need to be able to reason about the context in order to adapt to the specificities of as many homes as possible. They cannot rely on users or hard-coded objects, instead the location and search facilities of the context manager will be key to reasoning about the context and answers questions such as "give me all the lamp sources in that room" or "Have all inhabitants left home now?". In its current implementation, the context manager is starting to be able to provide an answer to this type of questions.

APPENDIX A
INTEGRATING WSN SENSORS AND ACTUATORS

Apart from the TinyNode deployment that has been described in section VII, additional Tcl scripts have been written in order to interface with IPv6-based WSN, one of the areas where the OS Contiki[22] is widely used. In meshing WSN, it is essential to restrict the size and number of packets to a strict minimum in order to keep power requirements low. The current implementation of these scripts relies on the HTTP capabilities of the motes. HTTP leads to sizable headers and the necessity to keep the TCP state across the network. Future directions will look into UDP[19] and WebSockets.

Scripts bridging motes to the context manager will receive or poll for mote data and push this data as updates to the field of one or several objects in the context manager. The simplest script will regularly poll for data at given motes with a given frequency. However, the more complex script is inspired by techniques initiated by CoAP[26]. It combines a UDP and HTTP servers, in order to both support regular HTTP POST and GET operations, but also to entertain WebSockets connections. On startup, the script contacts all relevant

Figure 9. Two of the supported motes. To the left is a mote from Tyndall[25] that sports a stackable and pluggable interface for various sorts of sensors (temperature and humidity on the picture). To the right is a commercial mote from Flexibility (see http://www.flexibity.com/) implementing a thermometer, hygrometer and barometer.

motes and subscribes itself (the proper root/details to the servers that it implements), together with a frequency for reception of data. Consequently, motes will, whenever needed push data to the script, which will forward it further to the appropriate objects of the context manager, depending on its configuration.

ACKNOWLEDGMENTS

Most of the work has been sponsored by the European ARTEMIS project me^{3}gas, with valuable input from M. Westbergh (CRL Sweden), S. Duquennoy (SICS), J. Eriksson (SICS), P. Kool (CNet), P. Hansson(SICS) and L. Moore (Tyndall). Most of the code has been opened source at the following project location: http://code.google.com/p/efr-tools/

REFERENCES

[1] B. Welch, K. Jones, and J. Hobbs, *Practical Programming in Tcl and Tk*. Prentice Hall, 20 June 2003.

[2] K. P. Birman and T. A. Joseph, "Exploiting virtual synchrony in distributed systems," in *ACM Symposium on Operating Systems Principles (SOSP'87)*, pp. 123–138, 1987.

[3] R. Fielding, *Architectural Styles and the Design of Network-based Software Architectures*, ch. 5, pp. 76–106. 2000.

---

[19]Problems with the current UDP implementations in Tcl 8.6 (and in combination with IPv6) have unfortunately put part of the development on hold.

[4] D. Crockford, "The application/json Media Type for JavaScript Object Notation (JSON)." RFC 4627 (Informational), July 2006.

[5] M. Banzi, *Getting Started with Arduino*. Make:Books, O'Reilly Media, Inc., Aug. 2011.

[6] S. Monk, *Getting Started with .NET Gadgeteer*. Make:Books, O'Reilly Media Inc., 4 May 2012.

[7] T. Berners-Lee, J. Hendler, and O. Lassila, "The Semantic Web," *Scientific American*, 17 May 2001.

[8] K. Aberer, M. Hauswirth, and A. Salehi, "A Middleware For Fast And Flexible Sensor Network Deployment," in *Proceedings of VLDB'06*, pp. 1199–1202, 2006.

[9] P. B. Gibbons, B. Karp, Y. Ke, S. Nath, and S. Seshan, "IrisNet: An Architecture for a Worldwide Sensor Web," *IEEE Pervasive Computing*, vol. 2, pp. 22–33, Oct-Dec 2003.

[10] D. Halvik, G. Schimak, R. Denzer, and B. Stevenot, "Introduction to SANY (Sensors Anywhere) Integrated Project," in *Proceedings of ENVIRONINFO*, Sept. 2006.

[11] P. Kostelnik, M. Sarnovsk, and K. Furdik, "The Semantic Middleware for Networked Embedded Systems Applied in the Internet of Things and Services Domain," *Scalable Computing: Practice and Experience*, vol. 3, no. 12, pp. 307–315, 2011.

[12] M. Gudgin, M. Hadley, N. Mendelsohn, J.-J. Moreau, H. Frystyk Nielsen, A. Karmarkar, and Y. Lafon, "SOAP Version 1.2 Part 1: Messaging Framework (Second Edition)." W3C Recommendation, 27 Apr. 2007. http://www.w3.org/TR/soap12/.

[13] T. Bray, J. Paoli, C. Sperberg-McQueen, E. Maler, and F. Yergeau, "Extensible Markup Language (XML) 1.0 (Fifth Edition)." W3C Recommendation, 26 Nov. 2008. http://www.w3.org/TR/xml/.

[14] G. Klyne and C. Newman, "Date and Time on the Internet: Timestamps." RFC 3339 (Proposed Standard), July 2002.

[15] E. Rescorla, "HTTP Over TLS." RFC 2818 (Informational), May 2000. Updated by RFC 5785.

[16] S. Sanfilippo and P. Noordhuis, "Redis," 2012. http://redis.io/.

[17] I. Fette and A. Melnikov, "The WebSocket Protocol." RFC 6455 (Proposed Standard), Dec. 2011.

[18] A. Presser, L. Farrell, D. Kemp, W. Lupton, S. Tsuruyama, S. Albright, A. Donoho, J. Ritchie, B. Roe, M. Walker, T. Nixon, C. Evans, H. Rawas, T. Freeman, J. Park, C. Chan, F. Reynolds, J. Costa-Requena, Y. Ye, T. McGee, G. Knapen, M. Bodlaender, J. Guidi, L. Heerink, J. Gildred, A. Messer, Y. Kim, M. Wischy, A. Fiddian-Green, B. Fairman, J. Tourzan, and J. Fuller, "UPnP Device Architecture 1.1," tech. rep., UPnP Forum, 15 Oct. 2008.

[19] J. Franks, P. Hallam-Baker, J. Hostetler, S. Lawrence, P. Leach, A. Luotonen, and L. Stewart, "HTTP Authentication: Basic and Digest Access Authentication." RFC 2617 (Draft Standard), June 1999.

[20] P. Leach, M. Mealling, and R. Salz, "A Universally Unique IDentifier (UUID) URN Namespace." RFC 4122 (Proposed Standard), July 2005.

[21] H. Dubois-Ferrière, L. Fabre, R. Meier, and P. Metrailler, "Tinynode: a comprehensive platform for wireless sensor network applications," in *Proceedings of the 5th international conference on Information processing in sensor networks*, IPSN '06, (New York, NY, USA), pp. 358–365, ACM, 2006.

[22] A. Dunkels, B. Grönvall, and T. Voigt, "Contiki - a lightweight and flexible operating system for tiny networked sensors," in *Proceedings of the 29th Annual IEEE International Conference on Local Computer Networks*, pp. 455–462, 20 Dec. 2004.

[23] S. Petai, "python-plugwise." Bitbucket Project, 20 Mar. 2011. https://bitbucket.org/hadara/python-plugwise/wiki/Home.

[24] D. Wolber, H. Abelson, E. Spertus, and L. Looney, *App Inventor*. O'Reilly Series, O'Reilly Media, Inc., 15 Apr. 2011.

[25] A. Lynch, K. Aherne, P. Angove, J. Barton, Harte S., D. Diamond, and F. Regan, "The Tyndall Mote. Enabling Wireless Research and Practical Sensor Application Development.," in *Adjunct Proceedings, Advances in Pervasive Computing*, pp. 21–26, May 2006.

[26] Z. Shelby, K. Hartke, C. Bormann, and B. Frank, "Constrained Application Protocol (CoAP)," Internet Draft draft-ietf-core-coap-12, IETF, 1 Oct. 2012.

Dr. Emmanuel Frécon is a senior researcher at the Swedish Institute of Computer Science (SICS). He received his Ph.D. from the IT university of Gothenburg in 2004. He has (co-)authored a number of articles in books, refereed conferences and journals, as well as edited a book in the field of computer science. Across the years his research interests have slowly shifted from collaborative virtual environments to ubiquitous computing, not forgetting ambient displays and novel interaction techniques. He strongly believes in the feedback loop between technology and users.

Dr. Emmanuel Frécon is also an entrepreneur and has co-founded two companies. He is on leave from his second company, JoiceCare, where he worked as a system architect and CTO. JoiceCare sells products for the elderly market: a SIP-based video telephone and a video-based supervision system. He also believes that industry and research have a lot to bring to one another and intends to alternate workplaces as opportunities present themselves.

WTK for APWTCL

An implementation of TK like Widgets for APWTCL.

A paper for the Nineteenth Annual Tcl/Tk Conference

Abstract

During first half year of 2012 APWTCL (the successor of itcl in javascript) has been implemented and based on the javascript version two additional versions have been implemented for better native performance: APWTCL (Java) for Android based handhelds and APWTCL (Objective-C) for iPhone. To have running something comparable to Tk for APWTCL, there was the decision to use wtk from Mark Roseman (https://github.com/roseman/wtk) as a base. This package splits up the administration and data of a widget to be handled with Tcl (snit classes and objects) from the representation (displaying on the screen), which uses native support from the environment it is running on. Original wtk was dedicated to support javascript only, my implementation inserts an environment independent message interface (using a string based protocol) in between and then uses native support for displaying and handling the widgets and events. The action handling on the events is done by passing the information back to the Tcl part, which is modifying the (Tcl side) data and calling Tcl callback scripts if necessary.

Contact information

Arnulf Wiedemann

Lechstr. 10

D-86931 Prittriching

Email: arnulf@wiedemann-pri.de

1 The Idea

Already during implementing itcl in javascript there was the decision to use wtk as the frontend for GUI building. WTK (WebTk) is a Tk like implementation of some widgets (frame, entry, button, label, checkbutton and canvas) and a rudimentary implemenation of a grid manager. It is based on the idea to separate the data and administration part of the GUI from the presentation part. The communication between the two parts can be done in different ways:

- Using a direct function call to the wtk client side functions

- Using a client/server solution which is running the client part (the presentation part in javascript) in the browser and the server part (the Tcl part) on the serving machine

The base for the above implementation is a snit class widget, which can create and administrate a widget. It is (from the comment of the implementation of Mark Roseman):

A 'generic' widget object, which handles routines common to all widgets like assigning it an id, keeping track of whether or not it has been created, etc. Purely for convenience, we also include some code here that manages widgets that use -text or -textvariable, though not every widget will do so.

The "mega"widgets like frame, button, entry etc. are built with snit classes, which delegate a lot of functionality to the widget base class. Again a comment from Mark Roseman from the implementation:

Stuff for defining different widget types here. Note that all widgets are expected to implement the "_createjs" method. This is called by the generic widget code, and should return a Javascript command that can be used to create the widget on the web side of things (i.e. calls routines in wtk.js).

Widgets that support -text and -textvariable are expected to implement the "_textchangejs" method, which is called by the text handling pieces of the generic widget code, and should return a Javascript command that will change the text of the widget on the web side to match the current internal state of the widget here.

Widgets that receive events from the Javascript side are expected to implement the "_event" method, which is passed the widget-specific type of event and any parameters.

Wtk.js is a set of functions building the base of the repesentation/displaying (client side) part.

Communication between the administrative side and the displaying side is done using two global procs:

- toclient

- fromclient

These classes and procs have been used to implement a running version in itclinjavascript using a few javascript classes to allow the direct communication with the interpreter written in javascript.

2 How the current version started

As can be seen in my presentation APWTCL at the 10th European Tcl/Tk User Meeting ths year and on the wiki page there has been a reimplementation of itclinjavascript based on JimTcl. This version was the first version wtk from Mark Roseman as an interface for handling basic widget support. Following that APWTCL (Javascript) version there was another implementation of APWTCL in Java for supporting Android smartphones and an implementation in Objective-C for support of iPhones.

When arriving at the point for building support for wtk widgets the first approach was to use the administrative part of wtk mostly as it was and to replace sending of javascript code to the displaying part by a generic message (string based) interface.

On the client side there should be a small interpreter for decoding the messages and for switching and dispatching to the appropriate functions for doing the displaying and event handling work.

This was first implemented for the iOS version, later on there was a port of that code to Java to support Android.

3 The Message Interface

For the message interface a simple string based protocol was implemented, which had the the message itself and the parts encoded as length and info parts. A Message is generally built similar to a Tcl proc call in having a command and some parameters for the command. The command is normally a class object and the first parameter is the action to be executed on a GUI element. The parameter is normally a handle for the GUI element to be worked on and the other parameters are additional info for the action like option and value pairs. The first character of the message shows the type of the message normally M and there will eventually be a type E for end of a message block. That way the protocol is extensible with other types. Right now there exist no other types.

The layout of the message interface is as follows:

M<length of message>:<message>

<length of message> is the length of the following message text (not including the ":") as an integer number

and a message is composed of 1 .. n parts with the following layout:

<length of part>:<part>

<length of part> is the length of the following message text (not including the ":") as an integer number

<part> is a sequence of printable ASCII characters.

These messages are interpreted on the client side (or the part which acts as a client for example some class methods).

Some examples:

M53:9:wtkclient11:createLabel4:obj120:label: Hello Chicago

M33:9:wtkclient7:newGrid4:obj05:grid0

M38:9:wtkclient4:grid5:grid09:insertRow1:0

M48:9:wtkclient4:grid5:grid03:row1:010:insertCell1:0

M70:9:wtkclient4:grid5:grid03:row1:04:cell1:011:appendChild7:widgets4:obj1

M47:9:wtkclient12:createButton4:obj213:Hello Chicago

M70:9:wtkclient4:grid5:grid03:row1:04:cell1:011:appendChild7:widgets4:obj2

M38:9:wtkclient12:createButton4:obj34:Quit

M70:9:wtkclient4:grid5:grid03:row1:04:cell1:011:appendChild7:widgets4:obj3

4 The Client Side

The client side is responsible for creating and displaying the GUI elements like a button or a label.

The implementation of the GUI part started with the iPhone version, the Java version was done some time later.

Some details of the client side:

The client side is implemented as a class with methods for the GUI elements and other parts. There is one object of that class instantiated at the beginning and when starting the application the implementation of the toclient and fromclient methods is defined.

Toclient encodes the message and uses the instantiated client object as the object and calls the decode message implemented there.

A reference to the fromclient method is set by an appropriate setter call to the client object.

The client side decode method decodes and interprets the messages sent via the message interface

For example for this message:.

M53:9:wtkclient11:createLabel4:obj120:label: Hello Chicago

After decoding we get a Tcl like list with the following contents:

{wtkclient createLabel obj1 {label: Hello Chicago}}

The first two parts build the client objects method to be called (after some mangling): wtkclientCreateLabel and there are two parameters: obj1 and {label: Hello Chicago} for that message.

As iOS and Java both can call class method using a text string with reflection/selectors this is the technique used.

Method wtkclientCreateLabel is responsible for creating a GUI element label with the text: "label: Hello Chicago"

First approach for crating GUI elements was, to use the native GUI elements available on iPhone namely the UI* classes. Using that approach, there is a rather limited implementation of a button and label support. Rather limited in that respect only means there is no completely compatible environment available as for a Tk Button.

Instead of a mouse click there is the possibility to hit the button using a touch screen event. When this event fires a native method is called, which in turn can call another method (in our case come method inside the client class. This method is implemented to forward that "event" to the Tcl wtk part in calling the fromclient method with parameters. Via that way the notification for an event is reaching the Tcl part, which in turn can handle the administrative part of the event and eventually is sending back some other message to be handled, for example to change the text of a button when the button is hit.

5 Different Approach for GUI Elements

Very soon the implementation reached a point (at least on the iPhone side) where it was obvious, that there is a lot of functionality missing, when looking for Tk like widgets. That might be partially because Apple wants to look all their GUI stuff look like they want it to be dispayed.

At that time some experiments with OpenGL ES started. OpenGL ES is a cut down version of OpenGL running on iOS and on Android and as part of WebGL in javascript for browsers too.

The experiments were based on the idea to use screen buffer implementation of OpenGL ES as a base for displaying pixels on the screen and to use some primitive functions of OpenGL ES like drawing a line or a rectangle or a polygon and filling some area with colors. For displaying text the idea is to use a freetype font implementation, also available for the iPhone.

Using that approach, it would be possible to use 3-D elements to be shown and also rotation of text would be very easy using OpenGL Es functionality.

As OpenGL ES is also used as a base for some games on iOS the guess was, that it should be fast enough for the implementation of a Tk GUI.

Having some small knowledge of OpenGL from the implementation of ntk_widget the decision was made to give OpenGL ES a try, to see, what can be done using that.

6 Use of OpenGL ES

The implementation of OpenGL ES for iOS (iPhone) has a rather simple interface to work with. There is an OpenGL graphic context, which can be used to display OpenGL ES primitives like a screen buffer.

OpenGL ES also offers primitives for drawing lines and polygons and to fill areas. Areas are built using for example triangles (there is no support for rectangles, which can be built using two triangles). Lines and triangles are built using vertices. There is an advanced interface available for using arrays of vertices for building graphics elements.

There were some successful experiments in building a Tk button using two triangles for the inner rectangle part and using a combination of some lines for building borders.

It is possible to add an event handling function to be called when a user fires a touch screen event in hitting at some point on the screen. This event also contains the x and y coordinates, where the event happen, Using that information and knowing where on the screen is the area of the simulated button it is possible, to detect when the touch screen event was fired inside the button rectangle area.

When the touch event happened inside the button area it is possible to emulate the Tk like press and release events of a button in setting different border colors for the four borders built using some lines. That way it is possible to make the button look sunken or raised. Depending on the touch screen event.

Experimenting with that implementation the idea came up to eventually use the ideas behind themed Tk (tile or ttk). Looking at the implementation of ttk it seems to be feasible, to implement some modified version of themed Tk widgets using OpenGL ES as the graphic context for displaying the stuff on the screen. Going that way, it would be rather simple too to rotate elements including text. For displaying text there are still some experiments necessary as there is nreal experience yet on how freetype2 fonts are supported on the iPhone (iOS). There is a port/adaption af freetype fonts called freetype2 from David Petrie for iOS and there if a ftgl library called ftgles also from David Petrie which can be compiled, but I was not yet able to make a demo running also it can be linked and started, but the display stays black. Seems to be a problem of adapting to iOS5, as the original was designed for iOS4.

The implementation of themed Tk functionality itself seems to be straight forward, just a matter of doing the work in Objective-C respectively Java.

During testing the implementation there were some problems in building rounded corners for button corners. There have been implemented some different algorithms, but without final success. There were always problems with rendering in getting something looking nice. There is some more time needed to find something suitable, as it seems to be possible looking at iOS button with rounded corners. It has to be found out, if there is a problem with the algorithms used or with OpenGL ES or how to use the same rendering as iOS UI functions/algorithms are using.

7 Status

It seems the suggested way is doable.

It also seems, that using OpenGL ES as the base is a rather platform independent way.

Making work freetype fonts and ftgles to be done.

The complete implementation of themed Tk support is not yet started, it should be relatively easy using enough time to do the work, as the existing implementation for Tk is available.

It seems not to be possible to use native fonts with OpenGL ES.

The implementation of the widgets using OpenGL ES commands is at the beginning.

There is the need for test cases..

There is also the need for examples/demos.

Tcl 2012
Chicago, IL
November 14-16, 2012

Session 2
November 14, 13:15-14:15

Toward RESTful Desktop Applications

William H. Duquette

Jet Propulsion Laboratory, California Institute of Technology

William.H.Duquette@jpl.nasa.gov

Abstract

The REpresentational State Transfer (REST) architecture includes: the use of Uniform Resource Locators (URLs) to place a universe of data into a single namespace; the use of URL links within the data to allow applications and users to navigate the universe of data; HTML/CSS for the presentation of data; a limited set of operations that are available for all URLs; multiple content types; and content negotiation when retrieving data from a URL. REST is primarily used in web applications; however, pure desktop applications can also benefit from RESTful concepts and technologies, and especially from the integration of web-like technologies with classic application software. This paper describes how REST concepts and technology have been used in the Athena simulation to present a vast sea of heterogeneous data to the user.

1. Background

The Athena Stability & Recovery Operations (S&RO) Simulation is a model of political actors and the effects of their actions in a particular region of the world. The region is divided into neighborhoods, in which reside various civilian groups. The actors have a variety of assets, including money, military and police forces, and means of communication, which they use to achieve their political ends. The extent to which they succeed depends on the attitudes of the civilians, which change in response to current events. The model runs for a period of months to years, and produces a vast quantity of data, all of which needs to be presented to the analyst in some form or other.

The Problem

Athena stores most of its data in an SQLite3 *run-time database* (RDB). In Athena V2.0 most data was made available to the user by taking the output of a particular database table or view and throwing it into a `tablelist`-based browser.[1] Such a tabular display is useful; but when the information about a particular entity, an actor, say, is extremely heterogeneous, one tabular display cannot tell the whole story. It is possible to collect together the information about the actor by looking across a number of tabular browsers…but not surprisingly our users thought that the application ought to be doing this for them.

If only there was an easy way of presenting heterogeneous data to the user, while taking advantage of relationships within the data as an aid to navigation….

The Solution

HTML/CSS is a powerful, well-understood means of presenting heterogeneous data to the user. Uniform Resource Indicators (URIs) are a powerful means of identifying specific resources to present to the user from within a vast sea of such resources. Links to URIs embedded in the data are a powerful means of allowing the user (or the application) to navigate the sea of data. The resource pointed at by a URI can exist in multiple content-types; through content negotiation, the client can retrieve the content-type that is most useful for its purposes. These have generally been used in web applications. However, there is no reason why these concepts cannot be fruitfully used in the desktop environment within the context of a single application with no network interfaces, when the application's data model calls for it.

2. The Desktop REST Architecture

HTML, URIs, and the rest of the web technologies described above were created to support an architecture called REpresentational State Transfer (REST) [2]; an application that uses REST is called a *RESTful application*. REST is a web architecture; this section describes how we have modified the basic concept to create a desktop REST architecture within our application.

REST: A Summary

A RESTful application, or client, accesses *resources*: collections of data, or indeed any kind of entity, by means of *Uniform Resource Indicators* (URIs), of which there are two kinds, *Uniform Resource Locators* (URLs), for resources that can be located and retrieved on-line, and *Uniform Resource Names*, which are unique names for entities that exist off-line.

The client accesses these resources by means of a handful of verbs, which in principle apply to all resources. In a traditional REST app, which uses HTTP for its transport, these are usually GET, PUT, POST, and DELETE.

The resources are provided to the client by a *server*, and the server provides the data in a form called the *content type*. Content types are typically expressed as MIME types such as `text/plain` and `text/html`. A single resource might be available in any number of content types, and the precise data returned for the resource might differ from one content-type to the next. (E.g., `text/html` contains structure in a way that `text/plain` does not.)

The client accesses a server using an *agent*. The client gives the agent the URI of a resource, and a verb, and the agent locates the server and accesses it on the client's behalf. In particular, the agent handles *content negotiation*: given the content types the client is prepared to handle, the agent works with the server to provide the resources to the client in the content type it would most prefer.

A resource's content frequently contains URIs linking to related resources. The client can make use of these URIs to navigate the sea of resources.

The most common content type is `text/html`, because it provides a way to display the resource data attractively and allows the user to navigate the data space by clicking on links. These days, HTML documents typically use Cascading Style Sheets (CSS) for formatting and Javascript for interactivity. In a Tcl/Tk application, naturally, Tcl replaces Javascript.

These concepts and technologies provide just the thing to display heterogeneous, highly linked data to the user.

Why Not a Web App?

The advantages of the REST architecture would seem to be an argument for implementing Athena as a web application, yet there are compelling reasons for not doing so.

- Athena already exists as a single-user desktop application; moving to the web would change the architecture considerably.

- Network interfaces come with security headaches. And although Athena is not classified, it is often used in classified environments where network resources are tightly controlled and security is taken *very* seriously.

- Ease of installation is key; we do not want to require the users to install a web server. We could work around the installation issue by embedding something like TclHTTPD in Athena; but that still leaves us with the security headaches.

- We've not been asked to, nor do we have funding to make such significant changes, or to come fully up to speed on robust, secure web applications.

Adapting REST to the Desktop

So the question becomes, how do we use these RESTful concepts in a desktop application? We need to:

- Define a set of URIs that give access to various application resources.
- Determine the relevant content types. We use standard content types like `text/html`, but also types relevant to the desktop environment, such as `tk/image` and `tk/widget`.

- Implement a content server, and an agent with which to access it. Because the server resides within the application itself, access can be synchronous; the protocol reduces to a set of procedure calls.
- Specify tools for parsing URIs. We use the uri package from Tcllib.[3]
- Create tools for generating HTML output. (Yes, I wrote yet another HTML-formatting module. It's just something I do.)
- Choose a widget for displaying HTML/CSS
- Implement a web-browser-like mega-widget on top of TkHTML 3.0.
- Implement other widgets that can take advantage of server content.

With the RESTful components added, Athena's architecture is as shown in the following diagram; the new components are shown with a shaded background.

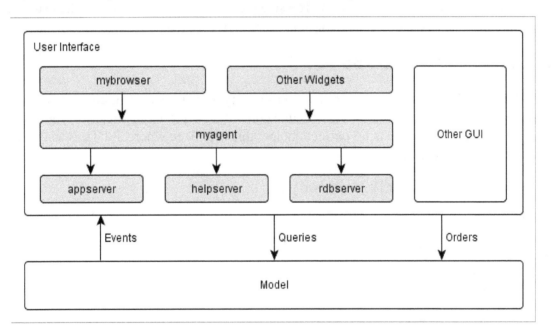

The Model represents the non-GUI portion of the application, including all management of scenario data and the simulation proper. As described in [4], Athena's User Interface interacts with the Model via three mechanisms. First, the UI can query the Model in any way it likes, provided that the queries do not affect the content of the Model in any way. Second, it can send *orders* to the model; all changes to Model content and operation are triggered by these orders. Third, the Model can send *events* to the UI, to notify it of particular happenings within the model. This portion of the Athena architecture remains unchanged from previous versions.

As a consequence of this existing architecture, we have not implemented the PUT, POST or DELETE verbs of the REST architecture; the existing mechanisms handle these operations perfectly well. Instead, we have focused on the GET operation, which is what we chiefly need to present information to the user.

At present, Athena includes three servers. The `helpserver` serves up on-line help pages from a pre-compiled help database. The `rdbserver` provides access to the schema and content of the application's run-time database as an aid to development and debugging. The `appserver` is the most important of the three, as it provides access to the Model's resources. These servers are all instances of the `myserver` type.

Each of these servers is registered with the `myagent` module; instances of `myagent` provide GET access to the servers, and also do content negotiation.

Instances of `mybrowser` can be used to browse the content of these servers in the usual way; and there are other widgets that access the servers as well.

3. Displaying HTML/CSS

Desktop REST stands or falls on the application's ability to display HTML content. And in order to display HTML content, or at least HTML-like content, in a Tcl/Tk application, you need to have an HTML widget. There is no perfect choice; this is a place where Tcl/Tk is sadly lacking. The available options are these:

- Solutions based on the Tk `text` widget

- TkHTML 2.0

- TkHTML 3.0 [5]

- A wrapper around Gecko or some similar engine HTML engine.

It is possible to do a mostly adequate job of displaying an early version of HTML in a Tk `text` widget; it handles links and interaction perfectly well, and it can even display images and embedded widgets. HTML-style tables are a problem, however, and tools to position images and embedded widgets precisely relative to the text (e.g., wrapping paragraphs around an image) are lacking. In short, the Tk `text` widget is a solution, but only a mediocre one for this purpose. (Were we to use it, we'd probably abandon HTML in favor of a Tcl-based presentation language, to avoid parsing.)

Athena 1.0 and 2.0 had a help browser based upon TkHTML 2.0. It is stable, having been abandoned long ago, but it is highly quirky and its HTML support is archaic. Font support is problematic; for example, you can have monospace type or bold type, but not both at the same time. It claims to support embedded widgets but in our experience all attempts to do so end in a crash. In our experience TkHTML 2.0 edges out the Tk `text` widget for display of rich content, primarily due to its support for tables, but it is not very satisfactory.

Another option is TkGecko [6], a Tk wrapper for Mozilla's Gecko HTML engine. It is clear from the TkGecko paper that Gecko is very much a moving target, and that wrapping it in a robust way is by no means easy. It would be an interesting choice if we wished to display live web content from over the network, but we do not; and stability is crucial.

TkHTML 3.0 is an HTML/CSS renderer implemented as the basis for a Tcl/Tk web browser. Abandoned some years ago, it has not kept up with the latest web standards. It has more than enough horsepower for displaying application data, however, including tables, embedded images, embedded widgets, and complex formatting. The bare widget lacks event bindings and other features that were provided by the web browser within which it was to be embedded, but once these are provided it becomes quite satisfying to use. It is fast, versatile, and sufficiently stable for our use, and is what we have opted to use.

4. The URI Scheme

Athena uses two distinct URI schemes, neither one of which is found in the wild: the `my://` scheme and the `gui://` scheme.

The `my://` Scheme

The most usual URI scheme used in Athena is the "`my://`" scheme, which is a simplification of the familiar `http://` scheme. `my://` URLs have the same syntax as `http://` URLs, with the unnecessary parts (port numbers, passwords, etc.) omitted:

```
my://server/path...?query#anchor
```

Here the server is the name of a `myserver` registered with `myagent`, and the path, query, and anchor are defined as usual.

We chose the name "`my:`" for this scheme because the named resource belongs to the application itself, rather than to some other entity out in the network. We considered abusing the `http://` scheme but rejected this for two reasons. First, we wanted to make it absolutely clear that Athena has no network interface; it is not pulling resources down from the web. Second, it allows us to modify the standards for `http://` URLs without causing confusion to future developers.

The `gui://` Scheme

The `gui://` scheme is a set of Uniform Resource Names (URNs) for entities in the Athena GUI. Links using this scheme are not handled directly by the `myagent/myserver` infrastructure; instead, the `mybrowser` widget hands them to its parent object via a callback, which hands to the application for handling. The upshot is that the user can click on a link in a browser, and the application will take them to some other tab in the GUI, or pop up an order dialog. For ease of parsing, the `gui://` scheme also uses a subset of the usual `http://` syntax.

5. Content Types

The `myserver` component allows each instance of the server to serve up content of any imaginable type. The standard MIME types `text/html` and `text/plain` are used for HTML and plain text context respectively; for consistency, application-specific content types are named in the same style, with "`tk/type`" used for Tk-specific content and "`tcl/type`" used for other kinds of data. The application-specific content types currently in use described in the following subsections.

The `tk/image` Content Type

The content consists of the name of a Tk image. An instance of `mybrowser` can display `tk/image` content directly and as the `src` of an HTML `<img>` tag.

The `tk/widget` Content Type

The content consists of a Tcl script to create the widget so that it can be displayed in an HTML page. The HTML `<object>` tag is used to embed widgets in pages; for example, the following HTML embeds a time plot in the page:

```
<object data="my://app/plot/time?start=2+vars=basecoop"
width="100%" height="3in"></object><p>
```

The query portion of the URL specifies the variables to plot, and the start time of the interval for which they should be plotted. The server uses these to customize the widget options, and then returns the script to create the widget. (The TkHTML 3.0 widget handles the width and height itself.) For example:

```
timechart %W -vars basecoop -start 2
```

The server doesn't know the window name to use, so it inserts a "`%W`" in place of the window name. The mybrowser substitutes in the window name and creates the widget, which then appears in the web page.

The Netscape Tcl plugin was never so easy.

The `tcl/enumlist` Content Type

This content type is simply a Tcl list of enumerated values; it is usually used to populate pulldowns in HTML forms, but can also be used by non-browser widgets.

The `tcl/enumdict` Content Type

This content type is similar to `tcl/enumlist`, but the value is a dictionary of enumerated values and their human-readable equivalents. It is also used to populate pulldowns in HTML forms.

The `tcl/linkdict` Content Type

This content type is used to represent trees of links. A `tcl/linkdict` is a nested dictionary mapping URLs (relative to the current server) to link metadata, primarily a human readable `label` and a `listIcon`, a Tk image to display next to the label. As such it represents one node in the tree, and its immediate children. By recursively retrieving `tcl/linkdicts` for the URLs, a component like the `linktree` widget can build up a tree of model entities or help pages.

6. Software Components

The Athena infrastructure includes the following software components.

The `myagent` Component

The `myagent` component is responsible for managing all interaction between clients and the various `myserver` instances. Servers register themselves with the `myagent` module, and instances of `myagent` retrieve data from the servers, doing all necessary URI resolution and content negotiation.

When creating an instance of `myagent`, the client specifies the content types it is prepared to handle, and the default server to contact:

```
myagent $agent \
    -defaultserver app \
    -contenttypes {text/html text/plain}
```

The client can then retrieve a URI's content as follows:

```
set cdict [$agent get $url]
```

The agent will throw a NOTFOUND error if the data cannot be retrieved; otherwise, it returns a dictionary with three keys: `url`, `contentType`, and `content`, which the client can do with as it pleases. If desired, the client can specify the desired content type or types explicitly:

```
set cdict [$agent get $url tk/widget]
```

Instances of `mybrowser` will normally accept `text/html`, `text/plain`, and `tk/image`, but will explicitly ask for `tk/widget` when handling an `<object>` element.

The `myserver` Component

Instances of the `myserver` component are registered with `myagent`, and thus become accessible to the application. Each instance of `myserver` defines the set of URLs that it can handle, and the content types for each:

```
myserver ::appserver
myagent register app ::appserver

appserver register / {/?}    \
    text/html [list /:html] \
    {Athena Welcome Page}

appserver register /actor/{a} {actor/(\w+)/?} \
        text/html [list /actor:html]           \
        "Detail page for actor {a}."
```

Each of these calls technically registers a pattern, rather than a specific URL; the handler handles all URLs that match the pattern. The first pattern registered above is simply "/", the top-level page for the server; the second registers a URL with a place holder for an actor's symbolic name.

For each pattern, we specify a unique name, e.g., `/actor/{a}`, and a documentation string; these are used in the server's `/urlhelp` page, which every instance of `myserver` provides automatically. Next, we provide a regular expression, which matches URLs of the correct pattern. (Note that "^" and "$" are added to the expression automatically.) The regular expression may include parentheses to indicate match parameters; these will be provided to the handler. Finally, for each URL we specify a set of content types and handler commands.

Thus, when the server is given a URI it matches it against the registered resources; if a match is found, and the URI has a compatible content type, the handler for that content type is called. For example:

```
proc /actor:html {udict matchArray} {
    upvar 1 $matchArray ""

    set actor [string toupper $(1)]

    if {![actor exists $actor]} {
        return -code error -errorcode NOTFOUND \
            "Unknown entity: [dict get $udict url]"
    }
    .
    .
    .
    return $content
}
```

The *udict* parameter is a dictionary of the components of the URI: the path, the query, and so forth, as returned by `uri::split`. The *matchArray* parameter is the name of an array variable containing the matches from the regular expression; in this case, the actor's symbolic name. The handler may make use of both the *udict* and the *matchArray* or neither.

The `mybrowser` Component

The `mybrowser` component is a web-browser-like widget built on top of TkHTML 3.0. It has its own instance of `myagent`, and thus can retrieve resources from servers. In addition to the normal browser navigation tools, it has the following capabilities:

- Display `text/html`, `text/plain`, and `tk/image` resources.

- Embed `tk/widget` content in `text/html` pages, when specified using the `<object>` tag.

- Support HTML forms.

The following figure shows an instance of `mybrowser`. The toolbar, scroll bars, html pane, and the paned window widget that allows the side bar to be resized, are all provided by `mybrowser`; the sidebar itself is an instance of `linktree` (see Section The linktree Component).

The browser's support for HTML forms is robust but idiosyncratic. Athena has its own set of data entry field widgets which do not entirely match up to the standard HTML form fields; consequently, it provides its own mapping of `<input>` types and attributes to data entry fields, ignoring the standard HTML input types completely. For example, this HTML creates a form consisting of a single "enum" field, essentially a pulldown containing items from an enumerated list. The list of values comes from URL `my://app/enum/sortby`, which must provide content type `tcl/enumdict`. The default value for the pulldown is "name".

```
<form action="my://app/page/Cal" autosubmit="yes">
<label for="sortby">Sort Cells By:</label>
<input name="sortby" type="enum" content="tcl/enumdict"
       src="my://app/enum/sortby" value="name">
</form>
```

The form looks like this in use:

Model Page: Cal

Sort Cells By: Cell Name ▼

When the form is submitted, which will happen automatically when the user selects a new value from the pulldown, the form's values will be appended to the `action` URL as a query, and the URL will be retrieved:

```
my://app/page/Cal?sortby=name
```

At present, `mybrowser` supports `enum`, `text`, and `submit` input types.

The `myhtmlpane` Component

The `myhtmlpane` component is essentially a `mybrowser` without the navigation controls. It is intended to display a single page, retrieved from a `myserver`, as an alternative to a window defined using normal Tk widgets. If the user clicks on a link on the page, the URI is passed along to the application for display in the application's main browser.

The linktree Component

The `linktree` component is a Tk treectrl widget configured to display a tree of resource links retrieved from a given URL. The widget retrieves its top-level items from the URL, and then works its way recursively down the tree, retrieving `tcl/linkdict` content at each node. The descent ends when a leaf no longer has any `tcl/linkdict` content associated with it. Optionally, the `linktree` can retrieve content for non-leaf nodes when they are first expanded.

The sidebar in the browser screenshot in Section The mybrowser Component shows a linktree of simulation entities.

The htmlframe Component

Although not actually part of the RESTful infrastructure, the `htmlframe` widget has proven to be a useful addition to the toolkit. It is simply a TkHTML 3.0 widget configured to layout its children according to an HTML layout string. For example:

```
htmlframe .f
ttk::entry .f.first
ttk::entry .f.last

.f layout {
    First Name: <input name="first"><p>
    Last Name: <input name="last"><p>
}
```

It includes a `set` method to set attributes of HTML elements by `id`; thus, the application can customize the appearance by setting CSS classes or styles on particular elements dynamically, or simply by providing a new layout. And since the TkHTML 3.0 widget supports scrolling, it is easier to create a scrolling window than it is using a standard `frame` widget.

This can be a much simpler way to create a complicated GUI layout than using the normal Tk geometry managers.

7. Status and Future Work

The infrastructure described in this paper is currently in use in two applications: the Athena simulation proper and in a separate development tool used to debug certain kinds of models. It has proven to be powerful, effective, and easy to use. The Athena application defines three servers and over sixty distinct URL patterns, many of them with placeholders. Many pages use forms and embedded objects, and that number is expected to increase over time.

It is possible that future applications may opt to extend the `myagent/myserver` pair with PUT, POST, and DELETE operations, and make use of these instead of Athena's existing "order" mechanism for editing and creating application data. Such an application would be truly RESTful, rather than merely "accidentally RESTful", as now.

8. A Bit of Advocacy

Tk needs a robust, solid, well-documented HTML widget for uses like those shown here, and the existing TkHTML 3.0 widget makes a good starting point. The secret is to stop chasing the big browsers; we will never have enough development horsepower to keep up with Mozilla, Microsoft, and Google, and even if we could produce a widget that was completely up to date and could display any HTML page on the web, it would be out-of-date in months, if not weeks.

But this is OK. An HTML widget need not be capable of doing everything Firefox does to be useful to the application.

9. References

[1]   Nemethi, Csaba, Tablelist Widget, http://www.nemethi.de/.

[2]   Sletten, Brian, "Resource-Oriented Architectures: Being 'In the Web'," in *Beautiful Architectures*, pp 89-109, 2009, O'Reilly & Associates, ISBN: 978-0-596-51798-4.

[3]   Kupries, Andreas, and Ball, Steve, uri URI Utilities package, found in Tcllib, http://tcllib.sourceforge.net/doc/uri.html.

[4]   Duquette, William H., "The State Controller Pattern: An Alternative to Actions", 17th Tcl/Tk Conference, http://www.tclcommunityassociation.org/wub/proceedings/Proceedings-2010/WillDuquette/Statecontroller.pdf.

[5]   Kennedy, Dan, TkHTML 3.0 Widget, http://tkhtml.tcl.tk/tkhtml.html.

[6]   Petasis, Georgios, "TkGecko: Another Attempt for an HTML Renderer for Tk", 17th Tcl/Tk Conference, http://www.tclcommunityassociation.org/wub/proceedings/Proceedings-2010/GeorgePetasis/TkGecko.pdf

10.   Acknowledgements

This research was carried out at the Jet Propulsion Laboratory, California Institute of Technology, under a contract with the National Aeronautics and Space Administration, during the development of the Athena Stability & Recovery Operations Simulation (Athena) for the TRADOC G2 Intelligence Support Activity (TRISA) at Fort Leavenworth, Kansas.

Tcl 2012
Chicago, IL
November 14-16, 2012

Session 4
November 15 10:45-12:15

KineTcl

Andreas Kupries ActiveState Software Inc. 409 Granville Vancouver, BC CA
andreask@ActiveState.com

ABSTRACT

This paper describes a package enabling Tcl scripts to talk to Microsoft's `Kinect` and related devices.

Technically `KineTcl` is a binding to the `OpenNI` framework and thus provides access to all depth sensor devices for which a sensor plugin exists. The best known device so far in that category is the `Kinect`.

The paper will describe the internal structure of the package (i.e. how it matches to the `OpenNI` API, and weaves both C and `Tcl` [12] together to make use of each others strengths) and point to supporting packages and tools used in the implementation.

1. OVERVIEW

`KineTcl` [2] is a new Tcl package providing a binding to Microsoft's `Kinect` [9], and related devices.

The project was started at the behest of the National Museum of Health and Medicine, Chicago[1] (short: `NMHMC`) for use in its exhibition space as one of the pieces of software linking real world activities and actions to interactive virtual displays.

Research into existing open source software for `Kinect` located two existing projects, `OpenKinect` [5] (aka `libfreenect`), and Open Natural Interaction (`OpenNI` [6]).

`OpenKinect` was created by the OSS and OSH communities through reverse engineering the Kinect's USB protocol. It is a low-level library providing access to the device without having to care about this USB protocol and the like. While not quite as low-level as a driver, it is not much higher. The developers have planned an analysis library for higher level operations (e.g. user detection and gesture recognition) but this was not yet implemented at the time of the research.

`OpenNI`, is a framework abstracting away from hardware devices and image processing for particular tasks (like user-, hand-, and skeleton-tracking). It was created and is maintained by `PrimeSense` [8], the developer and manufacturer of the depth sensor used in the Kinect. `OpenNI` is also "an industry-led, not-for-profit organization formed to cer-

tify and promote the compatibility and interoperability of Natural Interaction (NI) devices, applications and middleware." [6]. Both the framework itself and a generic sensor driver "node" for the `PrimeSense` sensor are available in source, under the LGPL. A derivative of the latter, specialized to the `Kinect` is available on github[10].

At this point of the research both possibilities were seen as roughly equivalent.

`OpenNI` was chosen because of the existence of the `NITE` [11] extensions, encapsulating all of the necessary higher level algorithms (i.e user detection, skeleton/joint tracking, gesture recognition, etc).

Given the time frame of the project (started in January 2012, a working system needed by May) it was considered difficult or impossible to invent and write such algorithms from scratch, as would be needed when using `libfreenect`. Having access to these through `NITE` outweighed the consideration that this part of the system is only available in binary, and not in source.

The next chapter gives a general overview of `KineTcl`'s design, implementation, and features. Following that, chapters 3 and 4 discuss limitations, possible applications and future directions for the package.

2. DESIGN & IMPLEMENTATION

2.1 OpenNI

`OpenNI`'s API is written in C, with an underlying class hierarchy [1] where the leaves represent the various data streams coming from a depth sensor, and the higher classes provide the general functionality and APIs. This is shown in figure 1. Note that the classes not only represent data streams from physical sensors, but also data coming out of higher level algorithms like user detection and tracking (i.e. virtual sensors).

These APIs contain the mandatory minimum supported functions for each class. For sensors going beyond these, `OpenNI` defines a series of standard "capabilities" they may provide. From a different point of view these could be called aspects, or mixins. As an example, figure 2 shows the capabilities which are defined for user detection and tracking.

For full details, see `OpenNI`'s reference documentation[7].

2.2 Basic Design

Generally all `OpenNI` classes and instances are represented as classes and instances to the Tcl script as well. Whenever

---

[1]Underneath the C API is actually C++

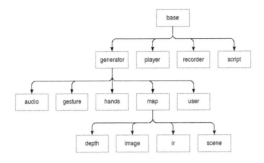

Figure 1: OpenNI class hierarchy

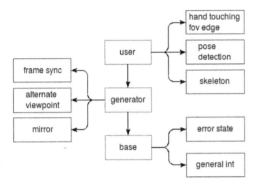

Figure 2: OpenNI User Tracking Capabilities

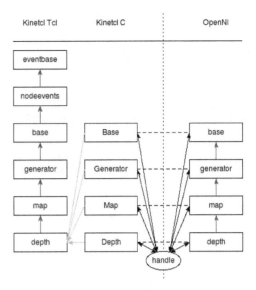

Figure 3: Package Layering

we mention a class in the future, we will also specify which of the three layers (`OpenNI`, C, or Tcl) we are talking about if it is not clear from the context.

Following the spirit of Poli-C [13] the binding is written using layers, with a low-level C layer implementing only the bare necessities which are then glued by the Tcl layer into the final user-visible API.

As mentioned, the C layer wraps each `OpenNI` "class" (which includes capabilities) into a Tcl class command whose methods map pretty much directly to `OpenNI` API functions. This is very much like Tk widgets. However, these classes do not know about the class hierarchy and superclasses. Each C class implements a binding to just the methods of their `OpenNI` class without regard for inherited methods.

This layering and the connections between the parts in the different layers is shown in figure 3, using the stack of classes for "depth image generator" nodes as example. We see not only the classes, but also the inheritance relationships (in blue), including the fact that `KineTcl`'s C layer does not use inheritance, and the use of instances (in red). The Tcl level depth image instances contain the C level instances of their class and all the required superclasses, which share the `OpenNI` handle for the node. This last point will be explained further in section 2.3.

This, and the mixin of the supported capabilities, is all handled in the Tcl layer. Here all the underlying classes are wrapped by `TclOO` [14] classes which instantiate all the required C classes so that the user may have access to the full set of methods, direct and inherited. The connection from the externally visible methods to the C methods is done through TclOO forwards, which also allows us to hide

all special C methods needed by the Tcl layer which are irrelevant from the user's perspective. This includes, for example, the various introspection methods used to manage callbacks/events and capability mixing.

2.3 Object Construction

One tricky point in all this is that the various C instances constructed for the Tcl instance all have to operate on a single `OpenNI` handle for the object in question (see figure 3). How do we disseminate this information?

First, only the leaf C classes can create a new handle, a property the binding inherits directly from `OpenNI`. Knowing that the Tcl glue will construct the leaf first then walk up the Tcl class hierarchy to construct the required C level superclass instances, the code for a leaf class saves the obtained handle into a per-interpreter structure of the package. The superclasses' code then retrieves the handle from there. Doing things in this manner avoids having to expose and pass a C level pointer through the Tcl layer.

It should be further noted that the C base class provides a special method (`@unmark`) to explicitly clear this handle store. This is not done automatically by the C base class during its construction, because of the capabilities. The handle storage has to be kept around until the Tcl glue has mixed them in, thus the responsibility to signal its release falls to the Tcl layer.

2.4 Object to Handle Conversion

Another issue which has to be solved in the cooperation of C and Tcl layers is that various `OpenNI` (and thus C) methods take a second handle as input, requiring us to convert from a Tcl object command to the underlying `OpenNI` handle.

At the C level, this is managed by calling out to the Tcl procedure `::kinetcl::Valid` which performs both validation of a Tcl_Obj* as a proper Tcl object (command) and its conversion, leaving the resulting `OpenNI` handle in the same storage area as used during object construction. The caller can retrieve it from there after the procedure returns.

At the Tcl level, `::kinetcl::Valid` uses a dictionary of the active instances managed by the base class to validate the argument as a Kinetcl object. For the arguments passing this test `::kinetcl::Valid` then uses its knowledge of the Tcl object internals, namely the existence and name of the C base class instance in the object to directly access it and invoke the special C method (`@mark`) which will store the desired handle in the storage area for the C level to pick it up from.

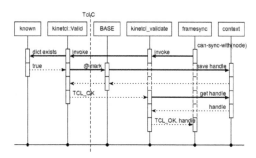

Figure 4: Object to Handle validation and conversion

Figure 4 shows all of the above in a UML sequence diagram.

2.5 Events and Callbacks

The last area of cooperation to talk about are the 34 `OpenNI` callbacks. Unfortunately, they are invoked from `OpenNI`'s internal threads, making it impossible to use them "as is" (i.e. let them directly call up into Tcl).

This issue was mainly solved by converting the callbacks into events, for which we have Tcl API functions to safely enqueue them regardless of which thread they come from and are going to. However, even with that we had two problems left.

First, one of the callbacks is very high-rate, generated several times per second. I am talking about the 'new frame' event for all the map generators, signaling the presence of a new image frame (image, depth, IR, ...). Because a single such signal is good enough this event is throttled by allowing only one per object into the event queue and discarding the remainder until the event in the queue has been processed.

The other remaining issue arises again from the fact that events are generated by threads outside of Tcl's control. It means that new events not only can, but will arrive while Tcl is processing the queued events. Without safeguards Tcl's event queue will never be empty, and the processing loop will never end, starving out idle-events processing.

While a solution was found for this, it doesn't look very nice. Readers of the example applications will see code like that shown in listing 1. This is essentially an emulation of Tcl's event loop using `while` and `update`, and inserting the necessary calls to (a) drive `OpenNI`'s processing (`waitUpdate`) and (b) safeguard (estart, estop) Tcl's event loop while processing events. `estop` causes the system to defer incoming events into a spill-over queue, whereas `estart` restores regular processing and moves all defered events into the main Tcl event queue.

With the pressure for getting a working system now gone,

Listing 1: Event loop
```
while {1} {
    kinetcl waitUpdate
    kinetcl estop
    update
    kinetcl estart
}
```

better solutions for the event integration should be investigated (e.g. Tcl's API for "Event Sources").

While `OpenNI`'s C API for callbacks allows the registration of an arbitrary number of actual callbacks for a specific event the C classes were kept simpler, handling only one actual callback per specific event, managed by associated set and unset methods.

The distribution of events to many observers is then again handled by the Tcl glue code, in two TclOO classes which are superclasses to the nomimal Tcl base class for `OpenNI` instances (see figure 3). These two classes, `kinetcl::eventbase` and `kinetcl::nodeevents,` provide a more event-like API, where users can `bind` to and `unbind` from events. The various Tcl sub-classes register the events they support with them, after using the C classes' method introspection facilities to determine this set. A small detail of the implementation is that a C level callback is set if and only if observers have been bound to the event it will be invoked for. This part of the functionality relies on a feature of the internally used `uevent` [15] package. That is, its ability to watch for and invoke commands when event bindings are set and removed (available since version 0.3.1).

2.6 Implementation

Now, how do we implement 39 C classes (14 core, 25 capabilities) quickly yet safely, especially in light of the large amount of virtually identical boilerplate needed to manage the class and instance commands and associated data structures?

By automating as much as possible.

Thus, a significant part of the time was not spent on writing the binding directly, but on writing the `critcl::class` generator package to encapsulate all the boilerplate and its templating. Having this generator in place, writing the binding became almost trivial, at least in most places. An only slighly abbreviated example is shown in listing 2.

Please note that the code in this listing represents the state of the Kinetcl head and of the `critcl::class` head officially released with `critcl 3.1 [4]`, which also makes use of the additional features for custom argument and result type processing.

The code currently in use by the NMHMC, found at the tag "nmhmc" in the `KineTcl` and `critcl repositories` is less streamlined, containing various argument- and result-processing C code fragments multiple times. For the class shown, the difference is only about half a kilobyte (4 versus 4.5 KB). This class gets converted into roughly 25 KB of C code. From this we can estimate that about 84% of the result is boilerplate code, generated, instead of manually written.

This was further simplified by agressively using Tcl's meta coding abilities to factor out the common parts of the various classes (leaf vs inner classes, the integer capability classes),

Listing 2: kinetcl::map implementation excerpt

```
critcl::class def ::kinetcl::Map {
    ::kt_abstract_class

    method bytes-per-pixel proc {} int {
        return xnGetBytesPerPixel (instance->handle);
    }

    method modes proc {} ok {
        XnStatus s;
        int lc;
        Tcl_Obj** lv = NULL;
        XnMapOutputMode* modes;

        lc = xnGetSupportedMapOutputModesCount (instance->handle);
        if (lc) {
            int i;

            modes = (XnMapOutputMode*) ckalloc (lc * sizeof (XnMapOutputMode));
            s = xnGetSupportedMapOutputModes (instance->handle, modes, &lc);
            CHECK_STATUS_GOTO;

            lv = (Tcl_Obj**) ckalloc (lc * sizeof (Tcl_Obj*));
            for (i = 0; i < lc; i++) {
                ...
            }

            ckfree ((char*) modes);
        }

        Tcl_SetObjResult (interp, Tcl_NewListObj (lc, lv));

        if (lc) {
            ckfree ((char*) lv);
        }

        return TCL_OK;
    error:
        ckfree ((char*) modes);
        return TCL_ERROR;
    }

    method @mode? proc {} ok {
        XnStatus        s;
        XnMapOutputMode mode;
        Tcl_Obj* mv [3];

        s = xnGetMapOutputMode (instance->handle, &mode);
        CHECK_STATUS_RETURN;

        ...

        Tcl_SetObjResult (interp, Tcl_NewListObj (3, mv));
        return TCL_OK;
    }

    method @mode: proc {int xres int yres int fps} XnStatus {
        XnMapOutputMode mode;

        mode.nXRes = xres;
        ...

        return xnSetMapOutputMode (instance->handle, &mode);
    }

    ::kt_callback mode \
        xnRegisterToMapOutputModeChange \
        xnUnregisterFromMapOutputModeChange \
        {} {}

    support {
        #define kinetcl_NUM_PIXELFORMATS (5)
        ...
    }
}
```

and generating the whole of the callback support from short descriptions as seen in listing 3.

Listing 3: Callback definition
```
::kt_callback user-enter \
    xnRegisterToUserReEnter \
    xnUnregisterFromUserReEnter \
    {{XnUserID u}} {
        CB_DETAIL ("user", Tcl_NewIntObj (u));
    }
```

This last was made relatively simple by the very regular nature of `OpenNI`'s API for the (de)registration of callbacks, including the callback signatures. Even the places where two or even three callbacks were managed by a single pair of (de)registration functions could be fitted in.

3. LIMITATIONS

A number of `OpenNI`'s features were not given full attention, or not implemented at all, because `KineTcl`'s intended use in the NMHMC did not require them. These are:

1. The audio, player, recorder, and script classes are mainly shells without full implementation. They are certainly not tested.

2. Instances are constructed using only default arguments. `OpenNI` actually has an API allowing the user to configure a query object/structure to limit the search for the type of instance to specific vendors, versions, and the like. None of this is used.

   Create a "user generator", for example, and the system will simply provide a handle it believes is the best.

3. Similarly `OpenNI` has functionality to query it for the set of installed modules, their vendors, versions, provided node types, etc. This also includes the ability to query what node stacks exist (i.e. coherent collections of nodes able to perform a task). For example, a "hands tracker" may need a "user generator" and if multiple modules provide implementations of either, `OpenNI` can construct different processing networks (node stacks) by mixing and matching them.

   None of this functionality is exposed by `KineTcl`.

4. FUTURE DIRECTIONS

Some of the things we can/may do in the future of `KineTcl` are obvious. Just look at the limitations listed in the previous chapter.

Another relatively obvious direction is to write additional processing classes directly in Tcl (e.g. implement various types of gesture recognition). Some work on this has actually been done, but is not complete (and buggy). See the files **stance.tcl** and **examples/dance** for the experiment with a **FAAST** [16] inspired system.

Finally, there is the currently used hack for the final integration of events. Better solutions for this, such as Tcl's API for "Event Sources", should be investigated.

APPENDIX
A. REFERENCES

[1] National Museum of Health and Medicine, Chicago http://www.nmhmchicago.org/

[2] Andreas Kupries, KineTcl. https://chiselapp.com/user/andreas_kupries/repository/KineTcl

[3] Andreas Kupries, CRIMP. http://wiki.tcl.tk/crimp

[4] Andreas Kupries, Steve Landers, Jean-Claude Wippler, CriTcl. http://jcw.github.com/critcl/

[5] Various. OpenKinect, libfreenect. http://openkinect.org/wiki/Main_Page

[6] PrimeSense. OpenNI organization and framework. http://www.openni.org

[7] PrimeSense. OpenNI API Reference. http://openni.org/Documentation/Reference/index.html

[8] PrimeSense. http://www.primesense.com

[9] Microsoft. Kinect. http://www.xbox.com/en-US/kinect/

[10] Avin. SensorKinect. https://github.com/avin2/SensorKinect

[11] PrimeSense. NITE. http://www.primesense.com/technology/nite3

[12] Various, Tcl. https://tcl.sourceforge.net

[13] Jean-Claude Wippler, Poli-C. http://wiki.tcl.tk/polic

[14] Donal Fellows, TclOO http://core.tcl.tk/tcloo

[15] Various, Tcllib. https://tcllib.sourceforge.net

[16] ICT, Flexible Action & Articulated Skeleton Toolkit http://projects.ict.usc.edu/mxr/faast/

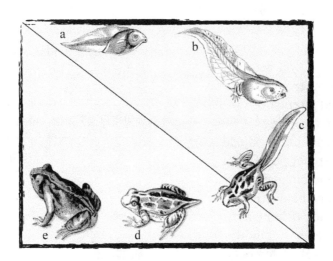

Lifecycle Object Generators (LOG)

Presented to the 19th Annual Tcl Developer's Conference (Tcl'2012)
Chicago, IL
November 12-14, 2012

Sean Deely Woods
Senior Developer
Test and Evaluation Solutions, LLC
400 Holiday Court
Suite 204
Warrenton, VA 22185
Email: yoda@etoyoc.com
Website: http://www.etoyoc.com

Abstract:

This paper describes a design concept call "Lifecycle Object Generators", or LOG for short. It involves a combination of coroutines, TclOO, and basic data structures to create objects that can readily transition from one class to another throughout the course of an application. This paper will describe the basic mechanisms required, and how this architecture can be applied to any complex problem from GUI design to Artificial Intelligence.

This paper is based on experience developing the Integrated Recovery Model for T&E Solutions.

Introduction

Most interesting computer models try to describe the actions and interactions of living, or at the very least animate, things. (The study of most dead an inanimate objects requiring a bit less computer power.) Living things have a tendency to change behavior. Until now modeling that change in behavior has required keeping track of state as variables and encoding every method with a patchwork of if/then/switch statements.

This paper will describe a new technique that exploits the ability of an object in TclOO to change class dynamically. TclOO is available as a package for Tcl 8.5, and is integrated into the core of the upcoming Tcl 8.6.

Style Guide

In this paper, I will be using the following style conventions:

Built in Tcl command/ keyword	`oo::class`
Name of an class, object, or variable	`class_bar`
Block of example code	`# Comment` `set foo bar`

Nickel Tour of TclOO

This paper exploits many advanced features of TclOO. But before we play with the advanced features, it may be helpful to go back over the basic ones.

A new class is declared with the `oo::class` command:

```
oo::class create classname {
 superclasses ancestor ancestor ...

 method methodname arguments {
  # Body of method
 }
}
```

Within the body, one declares the structure of the class. The keywords we'll be focusing on in this paper are:

`constructor`	Defines the constructor
`destructor`	Defines the destructor
`forward`	Forward calls for a method to another command
`method`	Define a method
`superclass`	Define the ancestors of this class

Once created, a class is a command. A command with several methods, the most important is `create`.

```
# Create a new object with a known name
classname create objectname

# Create a new object with a
# dynamically generated name
set obj [classname new]
```

And once an object is created, it lives as a command. To call a method:

```
objectname method $arg1 arg2 [arg3]
# Save a value returned from a method
set var [objectname method $arg]
```

If methods look and act a lot like procedures, that is by design. They can return a value, just like a standard Tcl proc. They can also call several built in commands, specific to the TclOO environment:

`my`	Exercise a method of the current object
`next`	Call on an ancestor's implementation of this class
`self`	Returns a the fully qualified name of this object

The **my** command is an unambiguous way for the Tcl parser to discern what commands are local to the object, and what commands should be resolved globally. It also makes for easier reading on the part of the programmer.

```
proc noop {string} {
  puts "global - $string"
}
oo::class create noop {
  method noop string {
    puts "[self] - $string"
  }
  method test {} {
    my noop "Hello World"
    noop "Hello World"
  }
}
noop create testobj
testobj test
testobj - Hello World
global - Hello World
```

In addtion to the **oo::class** command, TclOO provides **oo::define** and **oo::objdefine**. **oo::define** is used to modify a class dynamically. **oo::objdefine** is used to modify an object dynamically. TclOO also enhances the **info** command with two new methods: **info class** and **info object**, As you can imagine, **info class** provides introspection for classes, and **info object** provides introspection for objects.

Destroying a class

Classes in TclOO are implemented as objects, with their own constructors, destructors, and methods.

If you destroy a class, you automatically destroy any classes or objects derived from that class. And of course for every class that is destroyed as a result of destroying a class you destroy all of its derivatives, and so on. Taking our example from above:

```
info command obj*
obja objb objc objd obje objf
a destroy
info command obj*

# ^ Empty ^
```

Be careful though, *destroying objects by destroying their class prevents the object destructor from being called*.

Multiple Inheritance

One matter that will come up as we develop complex hierarchies of classes will be multiple inheritance. Given a choice between method implementations, TclOO will always choose the latest one defined.

```
oo::class create a {
 method noop {} { return a }
}
oo::class create b {
 superclass a
 method noop {} { return b }
}
oo::class create c {superclass a b}
oo::class create d {superclass b a}
oo::class create e {
 superclass c
 method noop {} { return e }
}
oo::class create f {superclass a b e}
oo::class create g {superclass a b c d e}
oo::class create h {superclass a b d c e}
oo::class create i {superclass e d c b a}
```

a is a common ancestor to the rest, and it provides an basic implementation of a method called *noop*. *b* is a descendent of *a* that provides its own implementation of *noop*. *c* and *d* inherit both *a* and *b* explicitly, but in a different order. *e* is a descendent of *b* that provides its own implementation of *noop*. *f* is a descendent of all of the classes *a-e*. *g-i* demonstrate various combinations of *a-e*.

```
foreach class {a b c d e f} {
 $class create obj$class
 puts [list obj$class [obj$class noop]]
}
obja a
objb b
objc b
objd b
obje e
objf e
objg e
objh e
obji e
```

You will see that in every example, the latest version of the *noop* that is defined is the one that is used. Since *b* is a descendent of *a*, given a choice between *b*'s implementation of a method and *a*'s implementation of a method, *b* will always be preferred. Likewise, *e* is a descendent of *b*. *e*'s version of a method will always be preferred to *b*'s.

If we do the example differently, sans b inheriting a and e inheriting b, we would get a different results, and the order in which classes are specified in the superclasses keyword becomes more important:

```
oo::class create a {
 method noop {} { return a }
}
oo::class create b {
 method noop {} { return b }
}
oo::class create c {
 superclass a b
}
oo::class create d {
 superclass b a
}
oo::class create e {
 method noop {} { return e }
}
oo::class create f {superclass a b e}
oo::class create g {superclass a b c d e}
oo::class create h {superclass a b d c e}
oo::class create i {superclass e d c b a}
```

```
foreach class {a b c d e f g h i} {
 $class create obj$class
 puts [list obj$class [obj$class noop]]
}
obja a
objb b
objc a
objd b
obje e
objf a
objg b
objh a
obji e
```

Objects Changing Classes

Within the `oo::objdefine` command is the ability for an object to change class:

```
oo::objdefine $object class $newclass
```

An object can even alter it's own class from within a method:

```
oo::class create moac {
 method morph newclass {
   oo::objdefine [self] class $newclass
 }
}
```

To demonstrate this process in action, imagine two classes, *classa* and *classb*:

```
oo::class create classa {
 superclass moac
 method testfunc {} {
   return "I am a classa object"
 }
}
oo::class create classb {
  superclass classa
  method testfunc {} {
    return "I am a classb object"
  }
}
```

Both classes have their own implementation of *testfunc*. The value that *testfunc* returns isn't as important as the fact that the values returned are different for the two different classes. Now with the help of a sufficiently rigged demo:

```
classb create test
test testfunc
I am a classb object
# Change class with oo::objdefine
oo::objdefine testfunc class classa
test testfunc
I am a classa object
# Ask the system what class test is
info object class test
::classa
```

```
# Change class with the morph method
test morph classb
test testfunc
I am a classb object
# Ask the system what class test is
info object class test
::classb
```

You can see that `oo::objdefine $object class` takes effect immediately. And it doesn't matter whether the call to change class occurs from within the object or externally. We can even change class several times during the execution of a method:

```
oo::define classb {
  method confusing_demo {} {
    # Store our present class
    set myclass [info object [self] \
      class]
    puts "Start"
    puts "1 - [my testfunc]"
    # Become a different class
    my morph classa
    puts "2 - [my testfunc]"
    # Return to our original class
    my morph $myclass
    puts "3 - [my testfunc]"
    puts "Done"
  }
}
```

The *classb* class now has an additional method, *confusing_demo*. Note, that through the miracle of modern science, changes to the class automatically apply to all objects that are instances of that class. So we can now call on this new method from our existing *test* object.

```
test confusing_demo
Start
1 - I am a classb object
2 - I am a classa object
3 - I am a classb object
Done
```

The body of *confusing_demo* is simply calling the same method three times. In between the calls, we change the class of the object with the *morph* method. The different implementations of *testfunc* give different output.

Beware of Disappearing Methods

There are plenty of ways to confuse matters by swapping an object's class. In this scenario, we have an event that is programmed to go off when an object changes class.

```
oo::class create  baz {
  method do_something {} {
    puts "Meh"
  }
  method morph newclass {
    oo::objdefine [self] class $newclass
    my do_something
  }
}
oo::class create  fubar {
  method event_morph {} {
    puts "I have morphed"
  }
  method morph newclass {
    oo::objdefine [self] class $newclass
    my event_morph
  }
}
```

Now, suppose we convert this object from *fubar* to *baz*:

```
fubar create test
test morph baz
error: Unknown method "event_morph"
```

We get an error! And we get that error because the object assumes the new class instantly. We just happened to pick a class that doesn't implement the *event_morph* method, which the script the object is running through tries to call on the next line.

Note, even though we encountered an error, *test* remains class *baz*. So if we run the *morph* method again:

```
test morph baz
Meh
```

It runs successfully. We can even make *test* back into a *fubar*:

```
info object class test
baz
test morph fubar
Meh
info object class test
fubar
test morph fubar
I have morphed
```

What Happens [next]

Another interesting wrinkle in changing classes is how the **next** keyword resolves within a method that changes the object's class. Lets say we have an class that uses **next** to exercise the ancestral implementation of the same method.

```
oo::class create a {
 superclass moac
 method testfunc {} {
   puts "a - [info object [self] class]"
 }
}
oo::class create b {
 superclass a
 method testfunc {} {
   next
   puts "b - [info object [self] class]"
 }
}
oo::class create c {
 superclass b
 method testfunc {} {
   my morph a
   next
   puts "c - [info object [self] class]"
 }
}
```

For interactions between *a* and *b*, things are quite straightforward.

```
a create test
test testfunc
a - a
test morph b
test testfunc
a - b
b - b
```

c is our complex case. Its implementation of *testfunc* changes the class of the object. And worse, it changes the class to one in which there is no ancestor for the **next** operator to hop to.

You would expect the system to die horribly along the lines of:

```
c create test
test testfunc
no next method implementation
    while executing
"next " ...
```

Instead we see:

```
c create test
test testfunc
a - a
b - a
c - a
# Note, the object really has changed
# class
info object class test
a
```

The pathway through the **next** calls is computed before the method is invoked.

Design Patterns

Now that we have covered the basics, it is time to start to develop the **LOG** framework.

Storing Properties

When an object expects to change class, there is often information specific to that class that we would like to access. A variable isn't a good fit for this purpose as its value doesn't change when the class changes. So I like to employ methods that return hard coded values.

The simplest way would be to declare a method for every value we would want to return:

```
oo::class create a {
 method color {} { return green }
 method flavor {} { return lime }
}
oo::class create b {
 method color {} { return green }
 method flavor {} { return apple }
}
oo::class create c {
 method color {} { return red }
 method flavor {} { return cherry }
}
```

For the lazy programmer this system has several drawbacks. First, it is difficult to distinguish between a method that is a property and a, shall we say, livelier method. Second, the notation is verbose. It introduces the temptation to cut and paste. Third, we have no fallback mechanism should a part of the system call for a property that has not been configured yet, or is simply not applicable to the object in question.

LOG adds two new methods: *property_define* and *properties*.

property_define creates a single value.

properties allow us to specify a key/value list. We can do this easily within TclOO because, behind the scenes, classes are merely a special kind of object. The just happen to be of class `oo::class`.

```
oo::define oo::class {
  method property_define {field value} {
    oo::define [self] method prop_$field \
       {} [list return $value]
  }
  method properties dict {
    foreach {var val} $dict {
      my property $var $val
    }
  }
  method property {field args} {
    set methods [info object methods [self] \
       -all -private]
    if {"prop_$field" in $methods } {
      return [my prop_$field {*}$args]
    }
  }
}
```

We also need to configure all of our client classes with a version of the property method.

```
oo::class create moac {
  method property {field args} {
    set methods [info object methods [self] \
       -all -private]
    if {"prop_$field" in $methods } {
      return [my prop_$field {*}$args]
    }
  }
}
```

So to configure a class:

```
oo::class create a {superclass moac}
a property_define color green
a properties {
 flavor lime
}
a create test
test property color
green
```

At the same time, if I ask for an item that is not configured (or configured yet), I get back an empty list instead of an error.

```
test property speed

# ^ Empty List ^
```

And if we are modeling a system worthy of a Lewis Carroll novel, we can alter the property of a class on the fly too.

```
a property_define speed very_fast
test property speed
very_fast
```

Using Classes to Represent State

State machine code becomes notoriously complex when there are more than a handful of states. I am going to introduce an easier way: create a separate class for each state an object can be in. Thus, if a method has to behave differently, we can just define that change for the particular state.

Let us begin with a few ground rules for changing an object's class. Even better, let's have a library of base classes that enforce those rules. All classes that are eligible to change class will be descendants of a common baseclass: *state_machine*.

state_machine provides several methods:

state_change	Change the class (and this state) of an object. Takes an additional argument which can pass additional data to event scripts.
state_current	Return the current class (thus state) of an object
state_enter	Script to run when an object enters the configured state
state_exit	Script to run when and object exits the current state

```
oo::class create state_machine {
  superclass moac ; # For "property" method
  constructor {} { my state_enter {} }
  # Return the current state
  method state_current {} {
    return [info object class \
    [self object]]
  }
  # Actions when we exit state
  method state_exit {} {}
  # Actions when we enter state
  method state_enter {} {}

  # Returns 1 if state changed
  # Returns 0 otherwise
  method state_change {newstate} {
    if { $newstate eq {} } { return 0 }
    set oldstate [my state_current]
    if { $newstate eq $oldstate } {
     # In the desired state, do nothing
     return 0
    }
    # Run cleanup from old state
    my state_exit
    oo::objdefine [self] class $newstate
    # Run setup from new state
    my state_enter
    return 1
  }
}
```

Example: Lifecycle of a Frog

Let is show off our newly developed *state_machine* with a demonstration: The lifecycle of a frog.

```
oo::class create frog {
  superclass state_machine
  method state_exit info {
    puts "Leaving [my state_current]"
  }
  method state_enter info {
    puts "Entering [my state_current]"
    next $info
  }
}
frog properties {
  has_tail 0
  respiration lung
  state_next {}
  color green
}
```

The baseclass *frog* is a series of general assumptions one could make about any frog, stored as properties. One of those properties *state_next* tells us what developmental state follows the current state. For an adult *frog*, we have no *state_next*, so we configure an empty set.

To model our frog's lifecycle, a program can simply walk from one state to another, reading the properties as it goes.

```
oo::class create frog.egg {
  superclass frog
}
frog.egg properties {
  has_tail 0
  respiration none
  state_next frog.tadpole
}
oo::class create frog.tadpole {
  superclass frog.egg
}
frog.tadpole properties {
  has_tail 1
  respiration gill
  state_next frog
}
```

```
frog.egg create hypno
set changed 1
while {$changed} {
 foreach fld {
   has_tail respiration state_next
 } {
   puts " * $fld [hypno property $fld]"
 }
 set newstate [hypno property state_next]
 set changed [hypno state_change $newstate]
}
Entering ::frog.egg
* has_tail 0
* respiration none
* state_next frog.tadpole
Leaving ::frog.egg
Entering ::frog.tadpole
* has_tail 1
* respiration gill
* state_next frog.tadpole
Leaving ::frog.tadpole
Entering ::frog
* has_tail 0
* respiration lung
* state_next frog
```

Discrete Time Phases

Discrete time simulations are similar to tabletop games. Actors (or players) take turns. And the rules of the game govern which interactions are valid during which part of a game turn.

In [1]Risk™ , each turn has three phases: placing reinforcements, attack, and fortifying. Players are only allowed to add troops to the battlefield at a certain time. There is only one phase in which we would expect troops to be removed from the battlefield (as casualties.) And there is only one point in the turn where troops can move. Phases make the outcome of a series of events more consistent.

Table games are engineered to have a definite "winner". The actor with priority is allowed to have a significant impact on the outcome of the scenario.

```
turn 1
 Player 1 - Reinforce Phase
 Player 1 - Attack Phase
 Player 1 - Fortify Phase

 Player 2 - Reinforce Phase
 Player 2 - Attack Phase
 Player 2 - Fortify Phase
```

With scientific simulations, we don't want a "winner." We want to devise a series of rules such that we get the same outcome whether the actors are run in sorted order, reverse sorted order, random order, or whatever that subtle, non-random, but sufficiently inscrutable order we get from [array names].

We also want to create the illusion that all of the actions in a given time phase occur simultaneously. So rather than let one actor run through all of the phases, followed by another, we give each actor an opportunity to act during every phase.

---

[1] Risk™, Trademark Parker Brothers

```
turn 1
 Player 1 - Reinforce Phase
 Player 2 - Reinforce Phase
 Player 1 - Attack Phase
 Player 2 - Attack Phase
 Player 1 - Fortify Phase
 Player 2 - Fortify Phase
turn 2
 ...
```

In simulators which allow objects to change class, I found it best to restrict any such changes to a specific phase in the time step. Preferably one in which nothing else is going on.

```
Agent Timestep
 phase_physics
 phase_observe
 phase_plan
 phase_action
 phase_reaction
 phase_morph
```

When an object wants to change state, the new state is recorded as a local state variable. The actual change does not take place until the morph phase comes around.

```
oo::define state_machine_discrete {
 method state_change newstate {
  if {[my state_current] eq $newstate } {
    return 0
  }
  my variable next_state
  set next_state $newstate
  return 1
 }
 ###
 # Called by the driver of the simulation
 ##
 method phase_morph {} {
  my variable next_state
  if { $next_state eq {} } {
   return
  }
  my state_exit
  oo::objdefine [self] class $next_state
  my state_enter
  set next_state {}
 }
}
```

Example: Agent Based Modeling

The Integrated Recovery Model simulates a ship and her crew during a shipboard catastrophe. Part of the simulation entails crew members changing roles. In the model, each role is represented by a distinct class.

Any number of events can lead to a crew member changing role. The most common role changes are in response to an order. Some orders are direct. For instance, a leader telling a crew member under his/her command "You do this." Other orders are indirect. When a crew member hears the call to go to General Quarters, he/she switches from whatever they were doing to their assigned role at GQ.

But the hardest ballet to choreograph by far was the transitions that occur when a crew member is assigned to a fire team. Most crew don't wear a fire suit as part of their regular duties. Thus a crew member newly assigned to a fire team must find a set of gear, put it on, and connect with a team that may already be on scene. Those behaviors were complex enough to merit a separate role.

```
Crew starts as role human
Crew receives order to join Team
 > Crew becomes role team.prospect
Crew member gathers equipment
Crew walks to location of Team leader
Crew joins Team
 > Crew becomes role team.member
Team battles fire
Team dissolves
 > Crew becomes team.dismissed
Crew returns equipment
Crew walks back to assigned station
 > Crew becomes human
```

In IRM, each agent is configured with a property that lists what tasks they want to perform, and in what priority. Each task, in turn, has criteria that govern when it should activate, when it should abort, and a coroutine to carry out once activated.

Our team.prospect class has the following task list:

action-station	Gather tools, report to action station
safety-check	Reflexes for fleeing from danger
join-team	Join the team we are assigned to
go-home	Return to action station (only called if join-team fails)

Every agent has an *action-station* task. It has a method that produces a list of equipment required for the role assigned. It checks to see that the agent has a working version of each. And if a device is missing, exhausted, or damaged, the agent gets a new one.

Normally agents produce their own list of needed equipment, based on information configured by the model maker. For this paper, the pseudocode uses a simple property.

```
agent::class human {
 method ensemble {} {
  return [my property equipment]
 }
 method ensemble_missing {} {
  set result {}
  foreach device [my ensemble] {
   if {[my device_working $device]!=1} {
     lappend result $device
   }
  }
  return $result
 }
 task action-station {
  begin {
    return [llength [my ensemble_missing]]
  }
  ... # Define the rest of the task ...
 }
}
```

```
agent::class fireteam {
  superclasses human
  properties {
   equipment { nfti scba ppe radio }
   member_equipment {scba ppe}
  }
}
agent::class rescueteam {
 superclasses human
 rescueteam properties {
   equipment { radio stretcher scba }
   member_equipment {scba medkit}
 }
}
# One team.prospect class suffices
# to join either team
agent::class team.prospect {
 superclasses human
 method ensemble {} {
  my variable team
  return [$team property member_equipment]
 }
}
```

Because the *team.prospect* role is it's own class, we can override the standard *ensemble* method with one that queries the team this agent will join.

```
# One team.prospect class suffices
# to join either team
agent::class team.prospect {
 superclasses human
 method ensemble {} {
  set team [my knowledge get team]
  return [$team property member_equipment]
 }
}
```

Thus:

```
fireteam create crew1
rescueteam create crew2
team.prospect create crew3
team.prospect create crew4
crew3 knowledge put team crew1
crew4 knowledge put team crew2
crew3 ensemble_missing
scba ppe
crew4 ensemble_missing
scba medkit
oo::objdefine crew3 human
crew3 ensemble_missing

# ^ Empty we are back to the human class
```

Application State

When designing a GUI, we also wrestle with state. Whether it be a megawidget, or a toplevel object that is managing the application, LOG can help.

In IRM our principle display interface is managed through a Tk canvas. Onto that canvas, we draw objects, color them, and respond to mouse gestures.

We divide our model's world into drawing layers. There are specific rules for rendering a wall that are different than, say, a piece of equipment. Likewise, a user double clicking on a wall expects a different dialog box if clicking a crew member versus a portal.

Window objects call out which layers are active and in which state as a method of the window:

```
irm::class modelwindow {
 superclasses [redacted]
 method active_layers {
   return {
    wall  layer.wall.basic
    compt layer.compt.basic
    portal layer.portal.basic
    eqpt  layer.eqpt.basic
    crew  layer.crew.basic
   }
 }
}
```

When devising a set of visuals, I put together two sets of classes. One is the application window, the other is a drawing layer that is modified to produce the visual.

```
irm::class modelwindow.damage {
 superclasses modelwindow
 method active_layers {
   return {
    wall  layer.wall.damage
    compt layer.compt.damage
    eqpt  layer.eqpt.damage
    crew  layer.crew.damage
    portal layer.portal.damage
    holes  layer.holes
   }
 }
}
```

In this case we are putting together a special mode that highlights damaged objects with a special color.

When applying a new state, the window object will call forth into being an object to represent each layer, and configured with the appropriate class. If the layer already exists it simply changes class.

In our example, the modified drawing layer colors all damaged components red.

```
irm::class layer.eqpt.damage {
 superclasses layer.eqpt.basic
 method node_is_damaged nodeid {
   # test for damage that returns 1 or 0
 }
 method node_style {nodeid} {
  if {[my node_is_damaged $nodeid]} {
    return {-fill red -outline -red}
  } else {
    return {-fill grey -outline grey}
  }
 }
}
```

Application window states can also specify bindings for the canvas. In the next example, upon entering the new state the canvas gets new bindings. Once the user clicks on an object the window translates motion to drag actions. When the user releases the dragged object, the window reverts back to its normal state.

```
irm::class modelwindow.drag {
 superclasses modelwindow
 method active_layers {
   return {
     wall  layer.wall.basic
     eqpt  layer.eqpt.editor
     crew  layer.crew.editor
   }
 }
 method state_enter {} {
   set canvas [my get canvas]
   bind $canvas <B1> \
     [list [self] drag_start %x %y]
   bind $canvas <B1-Motion> {}
   bind $canvas <B1-Release> {}
   my redraw
 }
 method drag_start {x y} {
  set obj [my object_at $x $y]
  if { $obj eq {} } { bell ; return }
  set canvas [my get canvas]
  bind $canvas <B1-Motion> \
    [list [self] drag_do $obj %x %y]
  bind $canvas <B1-Release> \
    [list [self] drag_done $obj %x %y]
 }
 method drag_done {obj x y} {
   set layer [my object_layer $obj]
   $layer move_to $obj $x $y
   my morph modelwindow
 }
}
```

Conclusion

Lifecycle Object Generators are not the solution to every problem in Object Oriented programming. But they are quite useful for complex state-based logic. I am developing these concepts into a fully featured toolkit, which is available for download at:

http://www.etoyoc.com/tcl

Image Credits:

Cover Image:
"Entwicklung des Krötenfrosches", By Meyers Konversations-Lexikon [Public domain], via Wikimedia Commons, accessed 17 October 2012, <http://commons.wikimedia.org/wiki/File%3AMetamorphosis_frog_Meyers.png>

Exploring Tcl Iteration Interfaces

By Phil Brooks

Presented at the 19th annual Tcl/Tk conference, Chicago Illinois November 2012

Mentor Graphics Corporation
8005 Boeckman Road
Wilsonville, Oregon
97070
phil_brooks@mentor.com

Abstract--- In Mentor Graphics' Calibre verification tool, Tcl is frequently used as a customer extension language - allowing customers to customize and drive the tool through various exposed interfaces. These interfaces are frequently used to access large collections of application data and provide a wide variety of mechanisms for iteration over that data. This paper will examine several interfaces that have been used for iteration over large C++ data structures along with the benefits and drawbacks of each method. Methods explored include Tcl lists, indexed array-like access, iterator object accessor (similar to C++ STL iterators), and specialized foreach style commands. Example stand alone implementations are provided and discussed from within the context of their original use in Calibre customer scripting interfaces. Ease of use and performance are considered.

1 Introduction

The simple task of iteration over each object in a container is one of the most common in programming. The task is so common that every programming language tends to develop common idioms for the form. Simple expression of the concept of iteration in a vernacular form aids readability and maintainability of code. In Tcl where the list is the most commonly used aggregate data structure, the foreach command is the standard for an iterative vernacular:

```
set test_list { a b c d }
foreach var $test_list {
    puts $var
}
```

When C based Tcl_Obj object interfaces that represent collections of underlying objects are being used, the foreach command itself is of little use since it works only with Tcl lists. So for iteration, either the Tcl object must convert its contents into Tcl list form, or another interface must be constructed for iteration over the object data sets. The remainder of this paper considers potential interfaces for this purpose.

2 Demo Environment

All of the demo interfaces used in the example program are providing access to the contents of a C++ array of doubles - or in C++ "std::vector<double>". A Tcl program is used to iterate over the contents and to accumulate a result which is returned to the C++ program. The context of the environment is that of a customized analysis routine that is called from the C++ application. The Tcl interface allows an end user to perform custom calculations without having access to the application C++ source code or having to manage a C compilation environment. The Tcl program has read only access to the C++ vector.

Since the Tcl routine is called directly from the C++ program, a record based user interface is provided so that the user can direct the application with the name of the Tcl script and the proc to call. In the Mentor Graphics Calibre environment, these Tcl calls are specified from the Standard Rulefile Verification Format (SVRF) language that makes up the bulk of the application's programming interface.

In this example program, a configuration file specifies the name of the Tcl script, a proc to call, and the iteration interface that is to be selected (from the 4 we are describing).

These fields are specified as simple text fields on a single line of the file:

```
<script_file> <called_proc> <interface>
```

For example:

```
list_user_script.tcl do_calculation list
```

describes list_user_script.tcl as the script file, calc_abmi as the Tcl proc, and the list generation interface as the interface to provide.

3 Loading the script file

After the config file is read, the script file itself is read and evaluated in the Tcl interpreter so that it can be called repeatedly as the application progresses through its data set. This is accomplished by first creating a Tcl_Obj that will contain the script:

```
Tcl_Obj* tcl_script = Tcl_NewObj();
Tcl_IncrRefCount( tcl_script );
```

(Note that code examples in the paper are sometimes slightly altered for brevity from the example program.) Then, the following code adds the script, line by line, to that object using Tcl_AppendStringsToObj:

```
std::ifstream file_loader( load_file.c_str() );
std::string load_line;
while( file_loader ) {
    std::getline(file_loader, load_line);
    Tcl_AppendStringsToObj( tcl_script,
        load_line.c_str(), "\n", NULL );
}
```

The script file itself is now loaded into the interpreter using Tcl_EvalObjEx:

```
rc = Tcl_EvalObjEx(interp,tcl_script,TCL_EVAL_GLOBAL);
```

Now the interpreter is ready to run the indicated proc for each vector in the analysis set.

4 Exploring the Iteration Interfaces

The main body of the paper explores several interfaces that an application can present to user through the Tcl C Tcl_Obj and Tcl_ObjType interfaces. The goal for these interfaces is to provide users simple and intuitive access to large native application datasets in an efficient manner that looks at least vaguely familiar and intuitive to Tcl users.

4.1 Accessing a Tcl List directly

The most natural and straight forward mechanism for iteration in Tcl is simple iteration through a Tcl list:

```
proc do_calculation input_list {
    # now iterate
    foreach var $input_list {
        puts $var
    }
}
```

The Tcl list is, then, a very straight forward mechanism to providing access to application data. The Tcl List interface is used in the Calibre product's LVS Device recognition application in order to provide access to a (usually) short set of numbers describing proximity of features near a transistor. Lists in the example program are constructed using the Tcl_ListObjAppendElement interface. The command is invoked by name (from the proc_name argument), with the list passed in the second field of the command:

```
//
// Tcl List construction from a C++ std::vector<double>
//
Tcl_Obj *command[2];
command[0] = Tcl_NewStringObj( proc_name.c_str(), -1 );
Tcl_IncrRefCount(command[0]);
command[1] = Tcl_NewObj(); Tcl_IncrRefCount(command[1]);
for( std::vector<double>::iterator i = data.begin();
    i != data.end(); ++i )
{
    Tcl_ListObjAppendElement(interp, command[1],
        Tcl_NewDoubleObj( *i ));
}
```

After construction of the list, the command text and the list are passed in to the calling script using Tcl_EvalObjv with the script text as the first argument and the list as the second argument.

```
int rc = Tcl_EvalObjv(interp,2,command,TCL_EVAL_GLOBAL);
```

Since the interface here is through a real Tcl list, this method presents the most natural interface to the Tcl programmer. Its main drawback is that the data structure must be fully copied from its native C++ into the Tcl list. For applications that have very large datasets, or high performance goals, the overhead required to form the Tcl list may be unacceptable. For those applications, the other access mechanisms may be more appropriate.

4.2 Access through an Index

The second interface demonstrated uses an index for random access into the contents of the container:

```
proc do_calculation my_arr {
    # returns an object count
    set entry_count [ $my_arr entry_count ]
    # iterate using an index
    for { set i 0 } { $i < $entry_count } { incr i } {
        puts "my_arr $i => [ $my_arr value $i ]
    }
}
```

The interface to the array is provided through the Tcl_CreateObjCommand interface.. In order to construct that interface, the example program uses Tcl's Tcl_CreateObjCommand interface.

```
Tcl_CreateObjCommand(interp,"arg1",
    vector_interface,data,NULL);
```

This call creates a command object named "arg1", bound with data pointer data, and implemented through the some_stats_vector_interface function. The name "arg1" is arbitrary and it is only used when inside the application as seen below. Inside the called proc, this command is bound to a parameter of the called proc. This technique allows the end user to select meaningful names for what are potentially a large number of parameters that all have real names that aren't very meaningful to the end user.

Next, the index_interface function provides implementation for the required commands:

```
int index_interface(
        ClientData cd,
        struct Tcl_Interp *interp,
        int objc,
        Tcl_Obj *CONST objv[] )
{
    std::vector<double>* data =
            static_cast<std::vector<double>*>(cd);
    const char* command =
            Tcl_GetStringFromObj( objv[1], NULL );
    if ( strcmp( command, "size" ) == 0 ) {
    f  size_t sz = data->size();
      Tcl_Obj *result=Tcl_NewLongObj(sz);
      Tcl_IncrRefCount(result);
      Tcl_SetObjResult( interp, result );
    } else if ( strcmp( command, "value" ) == 0 ) {
      ...
```

The object command is passed along with the name of the proc as an argument to Tcl_EvalObjEx. This is where the name "arg1" is used. It is not visible to the user (unless the user knows to look for it).

```
std::string invoke_line = procname;
invoke_line.append( " arg1" );
int rc = Tcl_Eval(interp,invoke_line.c_str());
```

The array index interface is used in the Calibre product's LVS Device recognition application in order to provide access to a randomly accessible array of measurement numbers related to a transistor. The advantage of this method over the constructed List method is mainly efficiency. The contents of the C++ vector are accessed directly by methods implemented through the Tcl_CreateObjCommand interface. The interface is not nearly as elegant as the list interface for simple iteration over the contents of a container. It also isn't suitable for data that doesn't fit an index->value retrieval model. The next interface extends the index to a more fully fledged iterator accessor.

4.3 Using an iterator interface similar to C++ iterators

The C++ standard library provides a convenient common mechanism for iteration through containers. That mechanism is called the 'iterator'. The code looks like this if you want to iterate through all members of an array of doubles called 'data' printing each item on a separate line:

```
std::vector<double>::iterator i = data.begin();
while ( i != data.end() ) {
    std::cout << *i << std::endl
    ++i;
}
```

We might construct a similar interface in Tcl where code could look like this:

```
set my_iter [ $data get_iterator ]

while { ! [$data at_end $my_iter] } {

    puts "my_arr $i => [ $data value $my_iter ]

    $data incr $my_iter

}
```

In the example program, the iterator interface is constructed from two parts. The record is accessed via a Tcl command object that is similar to the one used in the indexed interface. In the place of the index, the iterator is a full fledged Tcl_ObjType object. It can retain state and independent settings from the container itself. It is also more vulnerable to going out of synch with the container, so may require mechanisms to void its validity if the container changes state while the iterator is still in existence. The initialization of the command object is pretty much the same, using Tcl_CreateCommandObj, as it is for the indexed access. The commands supported by the implementation command are:

- get_iterator - returns an iterator to the beginning of the data container

- at_end - indicates the iterator is past the last data item in the data container

- incr - moves the iterator to the next item in the container

- value - retrieves the value represented by the iterator

The iterator itself represents the std::vector<double>::iterator and that is its only data member in this implementation. That is actually quite inadevalue quate since the vector iterator is represented by a raw pointer into the memory of the data vector. As long as the data vector remains in its original state, the iterator is fine. If the data container is altered or goes away, the iterator should, in fact, be invalidated immediately. This would normally be done with some sort of Observer pattern where the interface retains a list of active iterators and can void them when ever any operation occurs that would invalidate an iterator.

The Tcl_ObjType interface that contains the iterator pointer is implemented using the standard name and set of type handling functions for free, duplicate, update_string and set_from_any. These functions manage the access to the C++ iterator.

The iterator style interface is used in the Calibre product's Yield Server application to access a wide variety of EDA design data like electrical nets, devices, design cells, and geometries etc.

5 Exploring more consistent interfaces

The implementations explored thus far have resulted in vastly different Tcl code because of the mechanics of the underlying iteration mechanism and the fact that the Tcl foreach command is strictly a list-based iteration mechanism. In the next section, two methods of providing a more generic interface are explored. While the foreach command is strictly list based, a specialized foreach-like command can be used to soften the differences between the custom interfaces and the Tcl list interface. Coroutines, new to tcl, are also referred to as generators. They provide a potentially much more powerful and consistent interface to the problem of iteration.

5.1 Using a specialized foreach command

It is possible to adapt the interfaces presented earlier to get closer to the syntactic simplicity of the original foreach loop around the list. A specialized foreach-like command can be implemented that allows use of syntax that is very similar to the original foreach implementation on the list. The specialized foreach command can hide the differences between the various access interfaces allowing the user routine to The example program implements such a foreach_instance command on top of the indexed access method presented earlier. It does this with a specialized command "foreach_instance" which allows the following interface:

```
proc do_calculation record {
    foreach_instance value $record {
        puts $value
    }
}
```

which is very close to a Tcl List interface:

```
proc do_calculation record {
    foreach value $input_list {
        puts $value
    }
}
```

This foreach_instance command is implemented entirely in Tcl - and it hides the complexity of the index access interface. The foreach_instance proc is implemented as:

```
proc foreach_instance { var1 record body } {
    set vlen [ $record size ]
    upvar 1 $var1 value# now iterate
    for { set i 0 } { $i < $vlen } { incr i } {
        set value [$record value $i]
        uplevel 1 $body
    }
}
```

The foreach style top level command is used by the Calibre LVS Comparison application's device reduction application to give iterative access to a potentially large singly linked list of devices. While the two scripts are quite similar, they vary on the name of the critical foreach command itself. In the next section, use of a coroutine allows the difference to be obscured using another mechanism.

5.2 Using a Tcl coroutine with the index interface

Implementing a coroutine interface further explores the iterative style command in the context of coroutines. Using the coroutine, like the specialized foreach command, requires a specialized adapter routine that traverses the data structure for another command that is doing the calculation. One simple way to traverse a coroutine until it is empty follows. This example uses a coroutine to traverse a Tcl list:

```
proc do_calculation { record } {
  coroutine data_fetcher get_from_record $record
  while 1 {
    puts [ data_fetcher ]
  }
}
```

In this proc, the coroutine data_fetcher is created from the proc get_from_record (not shown) and its argument $record, the list of data. It then goes into a while loop that prints the value of each item in the list. The loop is broken when data_fetcher returns with a -code break return code that indicates the end of the list. Next is the implementation of a list iteration form of get_from_record:

```
proc get_from_record record {
    yield [ info coroutine ]
    foreach value $record {
        yield $value
    }
    return -code break
}
```

This calculation proc can remain unchanged while the get_from_record proc changes to cover a different interface - in this instance, the index interface shown above:

```
proc get_from_record record {
    set vlen [ record size ]
    yield [ info coroutine ]
    for { set idx 0 } { $idx < $vlen } { incr idx } {
        yield [ $the_record value $idx ]
    }
    return -code break
}
```

Tcl Coroutines are not currently used in the Calibre application family which is still using Tcl 8.4.

6 Conclusion

While Tcl provides a number of high performance adaptable interfaces to a C application programmer, iteration over a data collection is still quite cumbersome due to the differences in handling C object type collections and Tcl lists. These differences in interface are overcome in certain situations through the use of a customized foreach-like command, but that approach has a drawback in that the foreach-like command itself is specific to its data container. Coroutines provide promise for providing a common iteration mechanism within Tcl, though the language feature is new and idioms are not yet well developed.

7 Acknowledgments

Special thanks go to Donal K. Fellows for his assistance in writing the specialized foreach command and coroutine adapter interfaces.

Tcl 2012
Chicago, IL
November 14-16, 2012

Session 5
November 15 13:30-15:00

Pulling Out All the Stops - Part II

By Phil Brooks

Presented at the 19th annual Tcl/Tk conference, Chicago Illinois November 2012

Mentor Graphics Corporation
8005 Boeckman Road
Wilsonville, Oregon
97070
phil_brooks@mentor.com

Abstract--- At the 12th annual Tcl/Tk conference in Portland, Oregon, I presented a paper entitled 'Pulling Out All the Stops' - which concerned using Tcl as a user interface custom calculation engine at the heart of a high performance electronic design analysis package. This talk discussed the efficiency concerns and implementation details that were considered during implementation of this package. One simplifying constraint applied to the design was that, though this is a multi threaded application, a single Tcl interpreter was used and individual threads would access that Tcl interpreter through a mutex lock. seven years later, customers are running more complex calculation codes on systems with more processors. Locking on the single Tcl interpreter now restricts scaling. This paper briefly reviews the original design and then discusses the conversion to a fully threaded design in which one Tcl interpreter per thread allows completely parallel execution of the Tcl calculator.

1 Introduction - A review of the 2005 paper

The 2005 paper discusses implementation of Calibre LVS's Device TVF feature, in which a highly efficient, though quite limited, calculation engine is given the ability to make calls to a Tcl program allowing for more sophisticated programming capabilities. Some examples of the calculation language to Tcl calling mechanism is described. Finally, a set of implementation details that wring maximum performance out of the Tcl interpreter in this situation are described. Specifically, the major performance related recommendations were:

- Make use of `TCL_EVAL_GLOBAL`.

- The user's Tcl programs are pre-compiled before calculations are started using `Tcl_EvalObjv`.

- Runtime data access `Tcl_Obj` objects for arguments passed into function and return values are set up once up front and are reused during each individual call to the device calculator.

- Use Tcl object commands to hand off performance critical processing from Tcl to C++.

- End users are strongly encouraged to write compact efficient Tcl code.

The end of the 2005 paper includes a brief mention comparing Tcl 8.4 MT vs. Tcl 8.3 non MT builds and shows a favorable scaling improvement especially when 4 or more processors are used. The performance scaling that was visible in toy test cases, where the multi-threaded C++ processing was made as simple as possible and the Tcl processing was made artificially complex, bore no relationship to the real world testing on real customer data where the MT C++ part took vastly more time and the Tcl - even locked and single threaded - took hardly any time at all. So, the originally shipped implementation didn't use MT Tcl interpreters due to time constraints, tcl version constraints (we originally released on 8.3), some lurking bugs in the Tcl MT package, and one critical Tcl threading implementation detail that we had yet to uncover!

2 What has happened in the mean time

Over the next several years, customers started using the interface, at first in exactly the way it was designed... The original interface was conceived as a simple functional interface in which customers would pass in a couple of vector style parameters, run through a loop, perform the calculations of their choosing, and return a single value to the calculation engine to be used in later processing. We found that after they got used to the interface, customers did far more clever things than that with it:

- They would pass in dozens of parameters and make complex multi-step calculations.

- They would calculate several different parameters using the same set of input parameters, often doing preliminary calculations repeatedly due to the fact that our interface would only return a single number at a time.

- To get around the single return number constraint, customers would put together string results that were actually a concatenation of numbers separated by '_' characters and then pass them back and reparse those strings in subsequent calls.

We also found, during performance analysis on 16, 32, and 64 way systems, that, especially when customers did these sorts of complex calculations, the single shared Tcl interpreter was having a throttling effect on overall MT scaling of the application.

3 Searching for Clues

Most of the documentation that I could find for using multi-threaded Tcl talked about using Tcl itself to start and manage the threads. There is one passage in the book "Practical Programming in Tcl and Tk" by Welch, Jones and Hobbs [Welch] that says:

> *"At the C programming level, Tcl's threading model requires that a Tcl interpreter be managed by only one thread." p. 322*

And that's about it. The rest of the chapter talks about all of the facilities that Tcl has at the scripting level for creating and maintaining multiple interpreters using the Thread package, how to make them communicate with one another, how to pass channels back and forth, how best to write to a common file, how to share data efficiently between them, synchronization between Tcl threads, but nothing else that talks about how to run multiple interpreters that don't have to interact with one another from C. I didn't know it at the time, but that simple statement contains the most important thing (and possibly the only important thing) that you need to know to create independent parallel Tcl interpreters running on separate threads in C.

4 More about Calibre threading

Calibre has been a multi-threaded application for a very long time. There are embarrassingly parallel problems of computational geometry to be solved, and so they have been solved and improved upon since at least April of 1998. Here is an interesting CVS checkin log:

```
revision 1.1
date: 1998/04/10 17:41:31;
author: ****; state: Exp;
routines related to flat drc thread are going be in this
file. Currently there is not much in it.
```

Needless to say, there is considerably more in that file today than there was and the threading capabilities in Calibre are very well entrenched, so changing the threading model and control of the entire application for one new feature in the LVS is not in the cards. So years after the initial paper on 'Pulling out all the stops', it appeared, in fact, that more stops needed pulling, I rolled up my sleeves and resurrected the notion of running the Tcl interpreters in threads.

5 Task queue and thread pool Pattern

Let's look briefly at this commonly used pattern for threading architecture. The task queue and thread pool pattern [Wikipedia] is also known as the Worker-Crew Model [Sharapov]. In this pattern essentially separates the management of processing threads in a system from the tasks that need to be performed. This means that the threads can be managed for one set of constraints (like hardware availability, licenses, performance management, etc.) while task creation is under the purview of the application algorithms (like what things do I need to do and in what order do they need to occur).

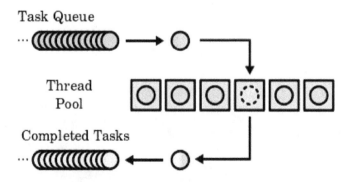

Figure 1. - Task Queue and Thread pool pattern - Wikipedia

Calibre uses just such a model for threading. This allows many disparate algorithms that may execute to solve a customer's particular problem to parcel their work out to a number of worker threads that complete the tasks according to hardware and licensing constraints that are managed by a completely different part of the system.

5.1 An Example Work Queue and Thread Pool API

So a work queue API generally has the following sorts of requirements and capabilities:

- it allows you to package up a unit of work including data and some direction for what needs doing.
- it allows you to ship that unit of work off to the work queue.

The thread pools then grab the pieces of work and execute them. At that point, the essential get-something-done part of the API comes in:

- it allows you to write some code that will do the work in a worker thread.

finally, once the work is done, the final piece:

- wake me up when its over.

5.2 Implementing work queue and thread pool in Calibre LVS

So, the Calibre device recognition algorithm follows the above prescription:

- In the main thread: Package up the work. Ship the tasks off to the thread pool.
- In a worker thread: Wake up and perform a task on a particular set of data.
- In the main thread: OK - wake up, everything is done now.

In my initial implementation, the following steps are taken in the main thread:

- Start setting up the algorithmic tasks. Ship the tasks off to the thread pool.

In a worker thread:

- Use thread specific storage to look for an existing interpreter
- if there is no interpreter create one. Also create the entire infrastructure for the interpreter, feed it the Tcl program text etc. Set up the argument objects, return objects, calling infrastructure etc. Store thread specific data inluding the pointer to the interpreter.
- Execute the local work task - it calls the thread's Tcl interpreter when needed.

At this point, everything is doing just fine. Now, once we finish all of the work, we need to clean up after ourselves.

- Wake up everything is done.
- Clean up the Tcl interpreters.

No big problem, just loop remember where all of the tcl interpreters are and delete them one at a time from the main thread!

5.3 Oops...

For the most part, the initial implementation worked fine. However, as this excerpt from my post to comp.lang.tcl points out, the cleanup at the end wasn't going so well:

> At the start of the processing that was requiring multiple Tcl interpreters, I set up some thread specific storage in a vector of pointers, then as each thread got its first task, it would check for an interpreter there if there was no interpreter, it would create one under its thread index.
>
> Threads would individually calculate, using Tcl and they ran nicely in parallel. At the end of the processing, once all of the tasks were done and the threads all quietly parked in their Calibre threading model parking slots, I would loop through on the main thread and destroy each interpreter. This is where things would go terribly wrong. Crashes, memory leaks, unclosed files, etc..

I finally reproduced the entire problem outside of my application in a small snippet of C++ and Tcl C api. While doing that, I found out that if I deleted the interpreter from inside the same thread that it was created in, all was fine, but if I did the same thing from the main thread in the same way that I was in the application, I got the same crashes that I had in the full application. I posted my findings to Comp.lang.tcl and received the following reply:

> Gerald W. Lester: ...

> *I also found that by deleting the interpreter inside the same*
> *execution thread that it was created in,*
> *Where else would you be deleting it from -- an interpreter is not supposed to be accessed*
> *by more than one thread. You may have many interpreters per thread (i.e. a thread can*
> *access/use many interpreters), but only one thread per interpreter (i.e. only a single*
> *thread should be accessing a given interpreter).*

Let's reread the bit from the book:

> *"At the C programming level, Tcl's threading model requires that a Tcl interpreter be*
> *managed by only one thread." p. 322*

Ahh - so that's what it means! I suggest rewriting that sentence:

> *"At the C programming level, Tcl's threading model requires that a Tcl interpreter be*
> *created, used and destroyed by only one thread. Interpreters cannot be used across*
> *multiple threads."*

6 Conclusion - Tcl threading from C Threads

Using Tcl interpreters in separate threads requires, absolutely, that the threaded interpreters be started (Tcl_CreateInterp) and stopped (Tcl_DeleteInterp) from within the thread that they execute in. This all makes perfect sense if Tcl is managing all of the threads in the application and lower level bits of code go off and do various low level things in a thread safe manner. It is a disaster if you are trying to plug Tcl into an existing threading system that uses the thread pool pattern in which you don't have control of or access to the individual threads, but instead submit tasks to a work queue that eventually dispatches them to threads.

Construction of the interpreters following this rule is fairly easy. Simple lazy creation of the interpreter from inside the execution thread and access through a thread specific variable or array slot works just fine.

Cleanup is much more problematic. Luckily, the guy that writes the work queue and thread pool code for Calibre LVS is just four doors down from me. Also, the architecture of our application is such that there are natural sequence points after each high level operation during which all of the threads are quiet. In Calibre, a new API that implements a "perform this task on each thread" routine which I now use to clean up interpreters. If we had a more heterogeneous work queue, though, this approach might not be possible. It would be much cleaner for this type of usage if

Tcl_DeleteInterp were able to clean up a quiet interpreter regardless of which thread it was created on.

Having found a solution to the Tcl threading issues, we can examine the performance of multiple Tcl interpreters doing user defined calculations in parallel on large numbers of parallel processors where we look for the next performance bottlenecks.

7 Acknowledgements

Special thanks to Fedor Pikus for helping me understand the pthread library more fully. Thanks also to Gerald W. Lester for his response to my initial query on comp.lang.tcl

8 References

"Practical Programming in Tcl and Tk" - Brent B. Welch, Ken Jones, with Jeffrey Hobbs, Prentice Hall, 2003
"Techniques for Optimizing Applications – High Performance" - Garg & Sharapov, Prentice Hall 2002 p. 394
"Thread Pool Pattern" - Wikipedia article

Brush: A New Tcl-like Language

Andy Goth

http://andy.junkdrome.org/

andrew.m.goth@gmail.com

November 2012[1]

This paper proposes a new programming language similar in structure to Tcl[2]. The new language embeds several functional programming concepts which are currently awkward or difficult to realize in Tcl. A reference system serves as the foundation for several other new features. The Tcl object model is refined to address performance concerns encountered in the Wibble[3] project. Syntax is fine-tuned to streamline preferred usage. Despite similarity to Tcl, backwards compatibility is broken. The paper discusses the motivation, design, and semantics of the language and provides a preliminary specification. Included code samples contrast how various tasks are done in Tcl and the new language.

---

1   This is version 3 of this document, released 20 November 2012.

2   http://wiki.tcl.tk/tcl Index of information on the Tcl programming language.

3   http://wiki.tcl.tk/wibble Wibble is a small, pure-Tcl web server.

Introduction

Tcl is a vastly powerful scripting language which blends deceptive simplicity with surprising functionality. Its minimal nature inspires programmer creativity, encouraging innovative designs difficult to imagine in more regimented languages. However, years of experience with Tcl have revealed its limitations, rough edges, and pitfalls which, while by no means fatal, could stand to be improved in order to empower programmers both experienced and new.

In the Cloverfield[4] project, Frédéric Bonnet[5] and I investigated possibilities for the next generation of Tcl. Though we shared many goals, we reached incompatible conclusions about the nature of the new language and decided to separately pursue our designs. As such, I cannot claim the Cloverfield name. For the time being, I will call my new language "**Brush**".

Brush has four primary design goals:

- Everything is a string.
- Streamline best practices.
- Enhance data structure access.
- Facilitate functional programming.

Brush does not attempt to maintain complete backward compatibility with Tcl. Several of its changes break existing scripts by subtly altering existing syntax and by defining new syntax using symbols and constructs not currently reserved.

This paper assumes a strong familiarity with Tcl script programming and a basic understanding of how Tcl is implemented.

At time of writing, Brush is **proposed but not implemented or formally specified.**

Everything is a String

One of Tcl's defining characteristics is its "everything is a string" philosophy, EIAS[6] for short. Brush embraces the Tcl EIAS philosophy without modification. EIAS informs the design of all new features in Brush. During previous iterations of Brush I considered and rejected features that conflicted with EIAS, and I redesigned others until they complied with this fundamental goal.

From the perspective of the programmer, EIAS means exactly what it says: Every value accessible within the Tcl interpreter is a string of text characters. This design offers a refreshingly natural way to program; the data is formatted in the same way it is described.

---

4   http://wiki.tcl.tk/cloverfield Cloverfield seeks to improve Tcl syntax and add missing features.
5   http://wiki.tcl.tk/fb Tcl Wiki page for Frédéric Bonnet.
6   http://wiki.tcl.tk/eias Discussion of the "everything is a string" concept and implementation.

EIAS offers many benefits:

- *Trivial serialization.* Strings are always suitable for transmission and archival.

- *Maximal compatibility.* Strings are a useful common denominator for all data types.

- *Easy introspection.* Displaying strings is effortless.

When a string follows a defined format, it can be said to be of the type described by that format. The important thing to notice about this definition is its fluidity: Types may exist within the imagination of the programmer, and strings can freely conform to many formats (therefore types) simultaneously. There is no need to declare types within the script. Typing is not an explicit activity; it is merely a convention, and type conventions may coexist.

Within a typical script, many types can be found: number, list, dictionary, script, math expression, regular expression, and of course string. These types all have distinct internal representations, as discussed below, but they are by no means the only types that can exist. Scripts may freely define new types built on top of existing ones; these are application-specific data structures. The definition is purely implicit in how the script chooses to access the data.

This is known as duck typing. If something walks like a duck and quacks like a duck, then it's a duck, even though it may also be a bird or a robot or a cartoon or a paranormal manifestation. Similarly, if values can be added together, they are numbers, though they are also valid as strings, byte arrays, regular expressions, and single-element lists.

Representations and Shimmering

Tcl and Brush use dual-ported values, meaning that at the C level they cache string and internal representations to avoid incessant conversions. Whenever a given representation is needed, it is either retrieved from the cache or generated from the other representation. For example, the first time a numeric value is printed, a string of ASCII digits 0-9 is generated and cached in preparation for the next time it is needed.

The dual representation design is invisible at the script level, except in rare usage patterns which induce a phenomenon known as shimmering[7]. Shimmering means frequently discarding and regenerating the string and internal representations, and it can sharply reduce performance, though it has no impact on correctness.

Shimmering becomes possible when the script repeatedly alternates its interpretation of a value's type. If the script switches between treating a value as a string and (say) a list, each time it modifies the value using one interpretation it invalidates the other cached representation, which must later be regenerated. Shimmering is possible even with purely read-only operations: When the script cycles between two or more non-string representations, e.g. between list and dictionary, each access displaces the previous internal representation since there is room for only one at a time.

---

7   http://wiki.tcl.tk/shimmering Shimmering is repetitive changing of the internal representation for some data.

Dict/List Unification

That last point touches on the first change Brush proposes to make to Tcl. No, Brush does not seek to add more internal representation cache slots; Brush retains the existing `Tcl_Obj`[8] structure which Tcl uses to store values. Brush's change is to unify the internal representations of lists and dictionaries. This avoids shimmering in the case of cycling between treating a value as a list and a dictionary, which is a legitimate use case experienced by the Wibble web server.

Wibble converts HTTP headers, queries, and POSTs to alternating key/value lists, which would be dictionaries if not for the possibility of duplicate keys. Tcl's [`dict`] dictionary commands ignore duplicates, so they are convenient when the website code does not expect duplicates, but in situations where duplicates are valid, the website code can instead use list-oriented commands such as [`foreach`].

EIAS requires a string representation to be generated when making a dictionary from a pure key/value list containing duplicates, since having only the dictionary representation would cause the duplicates to be lost. This duplication is very wasteful in the case of HTTP POSTs which may be megabytes in size. Having two representations doubles memory utilization.

Even in the case of canonical dictionaries (i.e. no duplicate keys), EIAS preservation incurs a performance penalty. Dictionaries are internally represented as hash tables for constant-time access, but standard hash tables are unordered, so converting a string to a dictionary and back scrambles the element order, thereby violating EIAS and the transparency of dual-ported values. Early versions of [`dict`] indeed had this problem. To correct it, the dictionary maintains a doubly linked list[9] chaining together the hash table entries in insertion order.

Tcl's implementation of dictionary values employs both hash tables and lists, yet it is not compatible with the implementation of list values. As mentioned before, alternating between [`dict`] and list commands results in shimmering, even when no write accesses are being done. It would make sense to combine the two to avoid shimmering and duplicate representations in the event of duplicate keys.

Nature of the Combined Type

The combined type is a list with an optional hash table index. The list component works just like current Tcl lists[10]: it is a linearly allocated array of `Tcl_Obj` pointers. The one change to the list structure is the addition of a pointer to an indexing hash table; if there is no index, this pointer is `NULL`. The hash table maps from keys (which, like everything else, are strings) to the indices of their corresponding values within the backing list. In this way, elements can be located in constant time either by index or by key.

---

8   http://wiki.tcl.tk/tcl_obj Tcl_Obj is the underlying data structure for all Tcl values.

9   http://core.tcl.tk/tcl/artifact/e62fccab713b5753edf37486f0947fa76bea265a Search for "`struct ChainEntry`".

10 http://core.tcl.tk/tcl/artifact/b3feb25636989d0d7d6b98f7814c01fac7e41b42 Search for "`struct List`".

In current Tcl, performing dictionary operations on a value causes its dictionary representation to be created if it does not already exist. In Brush, dictionary operations create a list representation (if needed) and construct a hash table index (if needed). One advantage is not having to discard an existing list representation; it is only necessary to augment it. Read-only list operations on a dictionary value do not need to do anything special, since it is also a list value. Using list operations to modify a dictionary value causes the index to be discarded, but the list representation need not be regenerated.

If a list value has duplicate keys, and its value is read via dictionary commands, the hash table index will simply omit all but the last of each duplicate. This results in the hash table index containing fewer than half as many elements as the list. (For canonical dictionaries, there is exactly one hash table index element for each pair of list elements.) Using dictionary commands to modify a non-canonical dictionary results in the duplicates being stripped; duplicates can be identified by not being present in the hash table index.

One drawback worth noting: Because the `Tcl_Obj` pointers are stored in a linear array, dictionary element removal takes linear time in Brush, as opposed to constant time in Tcl.

New Capabilities

Not all applications require dictionary keys to have values. Sometimes all that matters is whether or not a key is in the dictionary. This kind of data structure is called a set.

The usual Tcl implementation of a set is to make the keys map to dummy values, for example empty string. Lookup, insert, and delete all take constant time to complete, so the performance beats unsorted lists (linear time) and sorted lists (logarithmic time). The downside is that the string representation is littered with dummy values.

If the hash table index structure permits variable stride between key elements, it becomes possible to create a high-performance set structure with no need for dummy values. When the stride is two, the structure is a traditional key/value dictionary. With unit stride, the structure is a set.

Brush permits these two options, with the choice determined by which command is used to access the value. For key/value access, the traditional [dict] command is used. For sets, the new [lot] command is used.

A note on the name: [set] is taken, so I chose [lot] because it is a synonym of set and has similar pronunciation and spelling. Other possible names include: [ring], [field], [group], and [corpus], but I prefer [lot] because it does not abuse existing terminology. I am open to suggestions on the name.

Using a linear array to back a dictionary means that each element has a numeric index corresponding to insertion order. Classical sets are not ordered, but this feature is there in case a script needs it.

As with dictionaries, lots (sets) cannot contain duplicate keys, even though their backing lists can. Accessing a noncanonical lot with [lot] subcommands (described below) results in the duplicate keys being ignored, but they are visible to the list commands and are in the string representation. Any command that creates or returns a lot always produces a canonical lot, i.e. there are no duplicate keys.

One sample usage is in implementing enumerated types, whereby strings map bidirectionally to non-negative integers. Taking this a step further, a dense tabular data structure can be efficiently implemented as a list of rows, each being a list of cells, coupled with a lot mapping between column names and indices. The string representation would avoid the redundancy encountered when each row is a dictionary mapping from column names to cell values.

Proposed [lot] Subcommands

A functional programming style is more flexible and elegant than an imperative programming style; it frequently avoids the need for temporary variables which can clutter a program or collide with each other if not carefully named. Therefore most [lot] subcommands in Brush operate on values (as opposed to variables), return their results, and have no side effects.

The proposed functional commands are as follows:

Functional Commands Operating on Values	
lot contains lot key	True if lot contains key
lot create ?key ...?	Construct a lot given its keys
lot difference ?lot ...?	Symmetric difference of lots
lot empty ?lot ...?	True if all lots are empty
lot equal ?lot ...?	True if all lots are equal
lot exclude lot ?key ...?	Remove some keys from lot
lot include lot ?key ...?	Add some keys to lot
lot index lot index	Return index'th key in lot
lot info lot	Hash table statistics for lot
lot intersect ?lot ...?	Intersection of all lots
lot intersect3 lot1 lot2	List: (lot1 − lot2, lot1 ∩ lot2, lot2 − lot1)
lot search lot key	Return index of key in lot, or -1
lot size lot	Number of keys in lot
lot subset lot1 lot2	True if lot1 is a subset of lot2
lot subset -proper lot1 lot2	True if lot1 is a proper subset of lot2
lot subtract lot1 ?lot ...?	lot1 sans keys in subsequent lots

Functional Commands Operating on Values	
`lot superset lot1 lot2`	True if <u>lot1</u> is a superset of <u>lot2</u>
`lot superset -proper lot1 lot2`	True if <u>lot1</u> is a proper superset of <u>lot2</u>
`lot union ?lot ...?`	Union of all lots

For the sake of convenience, a few imperative commands are proposed which operate on variables given their references:

Imperative Commands Operating on Variables	
`lot set lotref ?key ...?`	Add some keys to lot named by <u>lotref</u>
`lot unset lotref ?key ...?`	Remove some keys from lot named by <u>lotref</u>

The organization of the [lot] subcommands may inspire a refactoring of the [dict] command, but that is not yet defined.

Enhanced Syntax

Tcl's syntax is simple, but that does not mean it's always simple to use. There are several situations where the simplicity of the syntax actually discourages safe, correct programming and instead leads novice programmers into bad habits. In other cases, the simplicity of the syntax leads to seeming inconsistencies which can only be deciphered once the programmer has developed an in-depth understanding of the language and its commands.

Brush proposes to give the Tcl syntax a face lift. The changes described below are not merely syntax sugar; they are intended to encourage the programmer to follow best practices[11] by making the right thing also be the easy thing. Other changes make the language less surprising in light of expectations established by other programming languages, plus there are a few neat experimental ideas.

Bridging Substitution and Command Contexts

The interpreter's goal is not to perform substitutions, it's to execute commands, and it only performs substitutions in order to assemble command lines. However, there are situations where substitution alone provides all the functionality needed, so the programmer wants a pass-through command whose sole purpose is to return its argument.

One such case is Tcl's new [lmap] command[12] which works like [foreach] except its return value is a list of results from each iteration of the script body. If the output list elements are to be made using substitutions, math expressions, or lists, it is necessary to use [subst], [expr] or [list], respectively.

---

11 http://wiki.tcl.tk/best+practices List of some best practices in Tcl.

12 http://tip.tcl.tk/405 The [lmap] command is a collecting loop with the semantics of [foreach].

However, [subst] and [expr] are dangerous if their argument is not brace-quoted to prevent double substitution. Also, Brush renames [list] to [list create] which takes longer to type.

The Tcl interpreter has long known how to do variable and script substitution and concatenation without the aid of a command, and Brush adds math expression and list constructor substitution (described below). Now that all these tasks can be done directly by the interpreter, it makes sense to offer a straightforward way to glue interpreter-driven substitution to commands such as [lmap].

Brush meets this need by providing a command that simply returns its first argument. The command is simply called [:] (a single colon), or the "pass-through command".

In this example, "$(...)" performs math substitution, and "(...)" constructs lists.

```
lmap (x y) (1 2 3 4) {: $(x + y)}        # 3 7
lmap f (y reas) {: And$f}                # Andy Andreas
lmap f (y reas) 1 (G K) {: (And$f $1)}   # {Andy G} {Andreas K}
```

For comparison, here is how the above is written in current Tcl:

```
lmap {x y} {1 2 3 4} {expr {$x + $y}}
lmap f {y reas} {subst {And$f}}
lmap f {y reas} 1 {G K} {list And$f $1}
```

The [:] pass-through command directly implements the K combinator[13], which returns its first argument and ignores its second, though scripts typically rely on side effects from computing the second argument. For example, here is postincrement. (The "&"s in front of variable names will be explained in the section on references.)

```
set &x 5                   # 5
set &y [: $x [incr &x]]    # 5
```

The return value of [:] is $x, which is substituted before Brush tries substituting [incr &x]. The return value of the latter is ignored, but that's fine since evaluating it had the desired side effect of incrementing the variable. In this example, "$x"'s final value is 6 and "$y" is 5.

For interactive use, [puts] and [:] have the same effect, though the mechanism is different. [puts] prints its argument to stdout and returns nothing, whereas [:] returns its argument to the shell which prints it to stdout. [:] is shorter to type and will be used in later examples.

Also to benefit interactive use, [:] returns empty string if given no arguments. This helps when running a command that will return a very large amount of data that would overwhelm the display. For example, typing the following line into a Brush shell will display nothing:

```
set &data [chan read [open hugefile]]; :
```

Math Expression Substitution

One of the secrets to Tcl's simplicity and flexibility is that it delegates nearly everything to commands. Like Lisp and Unix shell scripts, Tcl is command-oriented, not expression-

---

13 http://wiki.tcl.tk/k The surprisingly useful K combinator returns its first argument and discards its second.

oriented, and its operators (quoting, delimiting, substitution, expansion) exist to construct command arguments. Therefore, math is not a part of Tcl proper, but rather something that is done by the [expr], [if], [while], and [for] commands.

This is a good example of a little language[14] significantly extending the capabilities of the Tcl base language, which otherwise can only divide scripts into commands and words, performing substitutions along the way.

Yet, though this may be an interesting and consistent philosophical orientation, it has proven to be inconvenient for many practical programs. Math is needed very frequently, and in most programming languages math is "instantly" available: simply write the expression, and it's done. In Tcl, it takes an extra nine characters per math expression ("[expr {...}]"), plus a dollar sign for each variable usage.

One common shortcut is to omit the braces, saving two shifted keystrokes. In most cases this appears to give correct results, so programmers use it. However, it also creates serious performance and security problems. It hurts performance because there is no single Tcl_Obj in which to store the math expression internal representation, and it is insecure because double substitution[15] opens the door to injection attacks[16].

Brush improves the situation by making the safe, fast, correct programming style be the easiest to type. It introduces a shorthand for math expression substitution: "$(...)" is equivalent to "[expr {...}]", where "..." is any legal math expression. This reduces the per-expression overhead from nine characters to three.

The Brush interpreter performs no substitution on the text between the parentheses of "$(...)"; all it concerns itself with is locating the final close parenthesis. All math, including variable substitution, is performed by the math runtime, and there is no danger of double substitution.

This breaks compatibility with Tcl which interprets "$(...)" to be a directive to substitute an array element value, where the array variable name is empty string. (STOOOP[17] famously stores class and instance data in the empty-string array local to the object's namespace.) Consequently, Brush forbids using empty string as a variable name.

Brush retains the [expr] command for rare situations where the math expression (as opposed to any variables contained within) is legitimately dynamic, such as in a calculator application. To discourage abuse, automatic concatenation is removed; [expr] takes exactly one argument.

In addition to shortening the preferred syntax for performing math substitutions, in limited (but common) circumstances Brush relaxes the requirement to precede variable names with a "$" dollar sign.

---

14 http://wiki.tcl.tk/little+language In effect, each Tcl command defines its own domain-specific little language.

15 http://wiki.tcl.tk/double+substitution It is dangerous to reparse substitution results and do further substitution.

16 http://wiki.tcl.tk/injection+attack An injection attack is the substitution of executable code into an expression.

17 http://wiki.tcl.tk/stooop Simple Tcl-Only Object-Oriented Programming. Newer Tcl OOP systems exist.

If the variable name consists of only alphanumerics and underscores, and it does not start with a numeral, the dollar sign is optional. When using this shortcut, the variable must be named literally (i.e., no nested substitutions); it must not be named "eq", "ne", "in", or "ni"; and no indexing or dereferencing can be used. (See the section on substitution for details.)

These restrictions avoid ambiguity between variable substitutions, literals, function calls, array element names, and operators.

Any sequence of two or more ":"'s within or adjoining a variable name is treated as a namespace separator, not a ternary operator case separator.

Here are some examples and side-by-side comparisons:

Tcl	Brush	Description
`expr {cos($x * 2)}`	`: $(cos(x * 2))`	Cosine of two times $x
`expr {cos($arr(x) * 2)}`	`: $(cos($arr(x) * 2))`	Literal array index/dict key
`expr {cos($arr($x) * 2)}`	`: $(cos($arr($x) * 2))`	Index/key comes from $x
`expr $formula`	`expr $formula`	Dynamic math expression

List Constructors

In Tcl, the preferred way to construct a list from non-constant elements is with the [list] command. Each argument to [list] is an element in the returned list. The [list] command is crucial to any well-written Tcl program, but it is clumsy and therefore is avoided by novices who discover that double quotes are easier to type and give deceptively similar effects. Double quotes actually behave like [concat] which concatenates its arguments, collapsing one level of nested list structures, and corrupting the results when the elements contain spaces.

Even though I have coded Tcl for over a decade, I still sometimes look for ways to avoid [list]. Recently I had some deeply nested list containing almost entirely static data, but some buried element was variadic. Rather than code the whole thing using [list] so I could use a normal substitution, I used braces then applied [string map] to inject the element I needed. This is certainly not the most efficient implementation, but it is more readable despite its complexity.

Brush introduces a shorthand for [list]: parentheses. Parentheses at the beginning of a word behave like a new quoting mechanism. They nest like braces, but interior word boundaries are respected and substitutions are performed. There is no need for backslashes at the end of every line. The result is a pure list[18].

This shorthand provides an interesting possibility: reclaiming the [list] command for use as an ensemble. The [lindex], [lrange], etc. commands become [list index], [list range], etc. subcommands, organized the same as [string], [dict], and others. (The full complement of new [list] subcommands is not defined at this time.) The drawback is longer command

---

18 http://wiki.tcl.tk/pure+list A pure list is a value with list internal representation and no string representation.

names for common operations, but Brush also offers streamlined notation for list and dictionary access, discussed later.

Parentheses have no special meaning inside double-quoted and braced words, only at the "top level" of interpretation and nested within other parenthesized words.

The "{*}" expansion operator can be used to selectively force individual list elements to be split into multiple elements on embedded word boundaries. When "{*}" is used with every element in a parenthesized list, the effect is the same as if [concat] were used instead.

I envision this new notation being used for nearly all list construction. Brace quoting will be relegated to nested code (e.g., [proc] bodies and regular expressions) and for the interpreter-generated canonical representation of strings and lists requiring quoting.

Brace-quoted lists conflict with variadic elements, and the [list] command is a chore to type and visually clutters the code. The beginner temptation is to surround the list with double quotes, but this breaks when the substituted elements contain whitespace, mismatched braces, etc. Parentheses provide an attractive and sensible alternative.

Brush adds parenthesized lists not only to the main interpreter, but also to the math expression syntax. Within the context of a math expression, a list is constructed by surrounding it with parentheses and separating the elements (which are themselves general math expressions) with commas. To resolve the ambiguity between a single-element list and a simple parenthesized expression, a single-element list has a comma immediately before the closing parenthesis. The "{*}" operator is supported.

```
set &var (\$var value)        # {$var} value
: (     a      b c )          # a b c
: (a ( b c ) { d e } \{ ((
    )) " f g " $var)          # a {b c} { d e } \{ {{}} { f g } {$var value}
: ($var {*}$var)              # {$var value} {$var} value
: $("a" in ("a", "b", "c")}}) # 1
: $(($var, (1, 2), (3,), (),
"x y", ("x y",), {*}$var))    # {$var value} {1 2} 3 {} {x y} {{x y}} {$var} value
```

Sexagesimal Notation

For my work in geographic information systems, I frequently use sexagesimal (base-60) notation to express latitude and longitude. To date, I have not found any languages with direct or library support, so I have to implement it myself. It occurs to me that it might be a useful feature to have in Brush, serving as an alternate way of expressing a floating-point value. Sexagesimal is useful not only for GIS but also for timekeeping, since minutes and seconds are base-60 for time as well as angles.

Brush sexagesimal values are two or three nonempty strings of decimal digits separated by apostrophes "'". The value may have an optional "+" or "-" sign prefix. An optional fraction suffix may be supplied, consisting of a period "." and zero or more decimal digits.

The apostrophes divide the value into two or three fields, each of which is interpreted as decimal. The last field may have a fractional component. All fields except the first must be strictly less than 60.

When Brush encounters a sexagesimal value, it converts it to a real number by summing its fields. The second field is divided by 60, and the third field (if present) is divided by 3600. If the value has a "-" sign prefix, the sum is negated to get the final value.

Brush's [format] command gains a new "%D" conversion type which formats the value as sexagesimal. By default, or with the "h" (short) size modifier, the output has two fields (degrees and minutes). With the "l" (long) size modifier, the output has three fields (degrees, minutes, and seconds). The second and third fields are zero-padded to two digits. The precision specifies how many decimal places to give following the final field.

[scan] also gets "%D". With no size modifier, it autodetects the presence or absence of a seconds field. The optional "h" or "l" size modifiers explicitly specify the number of fields.

The mnemonic for "%D" is "degrees". It is chosen because it's adjacent to the sequence "%e", "%E", "%f", "%g", and "%G" which are Tcl's real number formats. Please do not confuse "%D" with "%d" which formats decimal integers.

Here are some examples demonstrating the various formats:

```
: $(1'02)          # 1.0333333333333334 %D   or %hD
: $(-5'02.300)     # -5.038333333333333 %.3D or %.3hD
: $(+10'02'03)     # 10.034166666666666 %+lD
: $(-89'02'03.45)  # -89.03429166666666 %.2lD
```

Comments

Tcl comments are quite different than those found in other languages. Most of the time they resemble Python, Perl, and Unix shell comments, but there are some subtle discrepancies:

- Even though Tcl comments continue until the end of the line, a closing brace will end the line, even if it appears to be inside the comment. (Syntax highlighters usually handle this incorrectly.)

- A comment can only start where a command could start, so it cannot go on the same line as another command without an intervening semicolon, and it cannot be placed inside a list.

Brush comments are designed to more closely match user expectations for scripting languages.

Brush's line comments continue to the end of the line, even if there are closing braces. This requires a major change to the brace counting mechanism, described in the next section.

There are situations where it is desirable to have both a comment and a closing brace on the same line, so Brush adds block comments which are akin to C's "/*...*/" mechanism. The notation for Brush's block comments is "#{...}#". Block comments nest, so they can be used to comment out large sections of code, even if they already contain block comments.

Brush offers more flexible comment placement than Tcl. Line and block comments can start wherever *any* word of a command can begin, not just the *first* word, so it is no longer necessary to precede the pound sign with a semicolon when the comment is on the same line as the code it documents. Comments can be embedded in parenthesized lists, not just scripts.

Comments are only stripped from parenthesized lists, not from lists quoted with braces, backslashes, or double quotes. This ensures two things:

- Comments are handled only by the parser, not the string-to-list conversion function.

- Braces, double quotes, or backslashes can quote a pound sign in a parenthesized list.

Here is an example showing how Brush comments can fit inside the last argument to [switch], which is a list alternating between patterns and scripts[19]. In Tcl, the comments can only go inside the scripts, but Brush also lets them go *between* the scripts when the list is constructed using parentheses.

```
switch $value (
    # first check option-*
    option-1 {puts something #{print something}#}
    option-2 {puts #{print the value}# $value}
    #{ comment this out until it's debugged...
    option-3 {putz oops #{mysterious error?}#}}#
    # now handle everything else
    default {puts "don't know what to do!"}
)
```

Block comments behave a lot like quoted words. The opening sequence "#{" is only recognized if it appears at the very start of the word, and it is illegal for any word characters to follow the closing "}#". Of course, the major difference between a block comment and any other kind of word is that it produces no output. In that sense, block comments are like empty string preceded by "{*}".

Brace Counting

Tcl novices are frequently surprised by brace counting. The current Tcl behavior is very simple: count any brace that is not preceded by an odd number of backslashes. While this works in most cases, it clashes with the C-inspired user expectation that braces in double quotes and comments do not count. Brush has a more sophisticated brace counting scheme that skips braces in quotes and comments.

Here is some faulty Tcl code that looks like it should work fine:

```
proc test {x} {
    if {$x} {
        puts "{"
    } else {
        puts "}"
    }
}
```

---

19 Thanks to duck typing, such an alternating list can also be thought of and processed as a dictionary.

Calling [test 0] produces no output because there is actually *no else argument* to [if]. This is because the braces within double quotes effectively "quote" the else. Calling [test 1] prints an open brace, then fails with "extra characters after close-brace", referring to the close quote following the close brace.

Within Tcl, the fix is to precede the quoted braces with backslashes. However, the need for extra quoting goes against user expectations and is therefore a common source of errors.

In Brush, braces do not count toward the open/close count when they appear inside double quotes. This corrects the specific problem experienced by the above code. The brace counter maintains a state machine tracking how each character and word it encounters will be interpreted during execution[20]. For example, if the first character of a word is a quote: start quote mode, so the word extends to the matching quote; in the interval, do not count braces.

Backslash-Newline

In Tcl, there is one surprising instance in which brace quoting modifies the word: backslash-newline. Within braces, if a newline is preceded by an odd number of backslashes, the backslash-newline and any subsequent spaces and tabs are *replaced* with a single space.

To date, I have not been able to find any justification for this behavior. At the top level (outside of any braces) the Tcl interpreter already knows to treat backslash-newline as a word separator rather than a command separator.

Brush removes this oddity in order to simplify line number counting and to ensure the return value of [info body] matches the actual source code.

Formal Argument Lists

A Tcl formal argument list binds actual arguments to variables inside [proc] and lambda[21] scripts. In addition to simply giving a name for each argument, it can supply default values for omitted arguments and store excess arguments in a catchall variable. These features are useful but have some restrictions:

- The catchall argument must be named "args" and can only be the last argument.

- Arguments with default values cannot occur before normal, non-default arguments.

- It is very difficult to tell if an argument was omitted or explicitly set to its default.

Brush removes these restrictions. Formal arguments can be placed in any order, the catchall argument can have any name, and an argument can be optional yet have no default value.

The syntax for Brush formal argument lists is a little different than used by Tcl. Optional arguments have a question mark "?" appended to their name, and the catchall argument (which does not have to be called "args") has an asterisk "*" appended to its name. These extra characters are not part of the variable name; they are notation for the argument list.

---

20 http://wiki.tcl.tk/cloverfield+-+parser Partial implementation of a similar parser made for the Cloverfield project.

21 http://wiki.tcl.tk/apply Tcl lambdas are anonymous procs and are executed using the [apply] command.

Brush adds another style of argument not found in Tcl, called a bound argument. Its value is hard-coded into the formal argument list and is unaffected by the actual arguments. In fact, the caller will never know the bound arguments are even there. Bound arguments are specified in the same way as defaulted arguments, except equal sign "=" is used instead of "?". Bound arguments are useful when programmatically generating procs that need to capture some of their environment at creation time.

Optional formal arguments *may* (not must) be specified as two-element lists, the first element being the name (with trailing "?") and the second the default value. If the formal argument is instead a single-element list, and the caller omits the actual argument when calling the procedure, the variable is not created. The procedure can check if the variable exists to ascertain whether the actual argument was supplied or omitted.

It is an error for there to be fewer actual arguments than there are non-optional formal arguments. It is also an error for there to be more actual arguments than formal arguments when there is no catchall formal argument.

Brush binds actual arguments to variables by simultaneously iterating through the formal and actual argument lists, considering them in pairs. The iterators are not always in lockstep.

The algorithm is as follows:

- Non-optional arguments are directly assigned to local variables with the same name as the formal argument, advancing both iterators.

- Optional arguments are assigned only if the number of remaining actual arguments exceeds the number of remaining required formal arguments. If they are skipped, the formal iterator advances but the actual iterator stays put.

- Bound arguments are assigned using the values in the formal argument list. Just like defaulted arguments, the formal iterator advances and the actual iterator is untouched.

- The catchall formal argument collects however many remaining actual arguments are in excess of the number of remaining formal arguments. If the argument counts match or if at least one optional argument is omitted, the local variable is set empty.

- At the end of the actual argument list, if any formal argument remain, they must be optional or catchall. They are set to default values or empty list, respectively.

These rules ensure all required arguments are assigned, then allots extra actual arguments to optional formal arguments (giving preference to earlier arguments in the list), then finally gives whatever is left to the catchall argument.

Many Tcl core commands (e.g., [lsearch]) take options at the beginning of the argument list, rather than the end. Brush's expanded formal argument list specification makes this easy to implement, plus it allows for the catchall argument to be called "options" rather than "args" if that makes more sense. Other commands take variadic arguments in the middle, for example [lset], which might choose to name its catchall argument "indices".

Not all Tcl core commands map nicely to the Brush model. For example, [puts] would be better served by assigning arguments right-to-left rather than left-to-right. In situations like these, the command can simply fall back on letting the catchall collect most arguments, then processing them however it wishes.

I conjecture that this new feature will improve performance since it reduces how much work the script must do to implement more complex argument schemes.

This table demonstrates the various types of formal arguments and how actual arguments are mapped to formal arguments:

Proc Definition	proc &p (a b? (c? xxx) d (e= yyy) f* g? h) {...}							
Proc Invocation	**Argument Value; "∅" If Variable Unset**							
	a	b	c	d	e	f	g	h
p 1 2	wrong # args: should be "p a ?b? ?c? e ?f ...? ?g? h"							
p 1 2 3	1	∅	xxx	2	yyy		∅	3
p 1 2 3 4	1	2	xxx	3	yyy		∅	4
p 1 2 3 4 5	1	2	3	4	yyy		∅	5
p 1 2 3 4 5 6	1	2	3	4	yyy		5	6
p 1 2 3 4 5 6 7	1	2	3	4	yyy	5	6	7
p 1 2 3 4 5 6 7 8	1	2	3	4	yyy	5 6	7	8
P 1 2 3 4 5 6 7 8 9	1	2	3	4	yyy	5 6 7	8	9

Multiple-Variable [set]

The first argument to [set] will always be a reference, which is distinct from any multi-element list. This makes it possible for [set] to also accept a list of references as its first argument, in which case it assigns to multiple variables at the same time. If [set]'s first argument has length greater than one, its second argument is treated as a list of values to be assigned in the manner of [foreach].

```
set (&a &b) (1 2)       #
: ($a $b)               # 1 2
```

Like Tcl's [lassign] command, Brush's multiple-variable [set] returns a list of extra values that were not assigned to variables. If all values were assigned, it returns an empty list.

```
set (&a &b) (1 2)       #
set (&a &b) (1 2 3)     # 3
set (&a &b) (1 2 3 4)   # 3 4
```

This is useful for shifting one or more elements from a list into variables, such as when processing command-line arguments.

```
set &args (1 2 3 4)
set &args [set (&a &b) $args]
: ($a $b $args)            # 1 2 {3 4}
```

To get this shift behavior for only one variable, use empty string as a dummy second variable:

```
set (&a ()) ()            # not enough arguments
set (&a ()) (1)           #
set (&a ()) (1 2)         # 2
set (&a ()) (1 2 3)       # 2 3
```

Unlike Tcl's [lassign], multiple-variable [set] throws an error when there are not enough values to assign to all variables.

Enhanced Index Notation

Classic Tcl string and list indexes are integers or "end" optionally followed by a negative integer[22]. TIP #176[23] adds support for "end+" followed by an integer and for two integers connected with "+" or "-". These new forms are intended to simplify basic arithmetic in situations where it would have been necessary to use "[expr {...}]".

Brush replaces this plethora of supported formats with the original three options, yet it meets the goal of TIP #176 with an alternate, more flexible approach: In indexes, integers are generalized to instead be arbitrary integer-valued expressions.

If "end" is used as a prefix, the expression must begin with "+" or "-", and the expression's value is added to the end index to get the normalized index.

Since it is an expression, the index must be brace-quoted if it contains substitutions or whitespace. However, Brush expressions do not always require variables to be preceded by "$", so braces can be omitted in many common situations.

```
set (&x &str) (2 abcdef)
string index $str 0        # a
string index $str end      # f
string index $str end-1    # e
string index $str x        # c
string index $str end-2*x  # b
string index $str end-1+1  # f
```

Substitution

One major goal for Brush is to provide the ability to name not only variables, but also individual dictionary or list elements within a variable's value. This minimizes the need for

---

22 http://www.tcl.tk/man/tcl8.4/TclCmd/string.htm#M9 String and list indexes have the same format.

23 http://tip.tcl.tk/176 This TIP adds simple index arithmetic capabilities to TclGetIntForIndex().

accessor commands. $-substitution is empowered to do the job directly, even for complex, nested, hybrid data structures.

Dictionary and List Substitutions

Brush borrows and extends the Tcl array notation, though it drops the underlying concept of a Tcl array, that being a collection of variables.

Dictionaries in Brush can be accessed using Tcl array notation, yet they otherwise work like Tcl dictionaries and are first-class objects. In addition to dictionary indexing, Brush offers list indexing, using braces instead of parentheses to surround the zero-based numerical index.

```
set &var (a b c d)
: $var          # a b c d
: $var(a)       # b
: $var{3}       # d
```

Indexing can be cascaded to navigate nested data structures, and the two styles of indexing can be mixed for hybrid data structures.

```
set &nums (en (zero one two) fr (zéro un deux))
: $nums          # en {zero one two} fr {zéro un deux}
: $nums(en)      # zero one two
: $nums(en){1}   # one
: $nums(fr){2}   # deux
```

Substitutions can be nested for indirection.

```
set &lang fr
: $nums($lang)      # zéro un deux
: $nums($lang){0}   # zéro
```

Indexed substitutions can be nested arbitrarily.

```
set &prefs (color blue lang en style classic)
set &rev (cero 0 uno 1 dos 2)
: $nums($prefs(lang)){$rev(dos)}    # two
```

Consecutive uses of a single style of indexing can be expressed either with multiple applications of the basic index notation or by giving an index "path" as a list within a single pair of parentheses or braces.

```
set &matrix ((0 5) (-5 0))
: $matrix{1}{0}                              # -5
: $matrix{1 0}                               # -5
set &contacts (bob (phone 555-1235 email bob@heaven.af.mil))
: $contacts(bob)(phone)           # 555-0216
: $contacts(bob phone)            # 555-0216
```

If such an index path comes from a substitution, it must be preceded by the "{*}" expansion operator, or it will be interpreted as a single index. As when constructing command arguments or a parenthesized list, "{*}" is equivalent to explicitly substituting in each list element in sequence.

```
set &rowcol (1 0)
: $matrix{$rowcol{0} $rowcol{1}}       # -5
: $matrix{{*}$rowcol}                  # -5
set &lookup (bob phone)
: $contacts($lookup{0} $lookup{1})  # 555-0216
: $contacts({*}$lookup)             # 555-0216
```

The text between list index braces and dictionary index parentheses is treated as a list. Care must be taken when performing dictionary indexing using a literally specified key which is a list with non-unit length or is not a well-formed list. Such keys must be quoted with double quotes, braces, backslashes, or parentheses. If the key is the result of substitution, there is no danger; it is a single index by default, unless "{*}" is used.

```
set &flatmatrix ((0 0) 0 (0 1) 5 (1 0) -5 (1 1) 0)
: $flatmatrix((1 0))                   # -5
set &contacts ("andy g" (email andrew.m.goth@gmail.com) "andreas k" (email ...))
: $contacts("andy g" email)      # andrew.m.goth@gmail.com
```

When a Brush list index substitution goes out of bounds, an error is generated. This is in contrast to Tcl [lindex] which returns empty string. Like Tcl [dict get], dictionary index substitution produces an error when the requested keys are not found.

If a programmer wants to follow a variable substitution with a literal "(", "{", or "@", he or she must use a backslash "\" to prevent the interpreter from interpreting the metacharacter. ("@" will be discussed later.)

```
set &user andygoth
set &host facebook.com
: $user\@$host        # andygoth@facebook.com
```

One feature not provided is the ability for a single path value to contain both dictionary and list indices. I cannot see a practical reason to build this into the language. If this feature is desired, a script can implement its own traversal mechanism:

```
proc &index (value path*) {
    foreach (&type &subpath) $path {
        switch $type (
            dict {set &value $value({*}$subpath)}
            list {set &value $value{{*}$subpath}}
        )
    }
    return $value
}
set &value (
    a (b ((x _ ) (y *) (z @ w ?)))
    c (d ((x \$)) e ((z \# w !) (z ~ w `)))
)
index $value dict (a b) list (2) dict (z)   # @
index $value list (1 0)                      # b
index $value dict (c d) list (0) dict (x)   # $
index $value list (3 3 0) dict (w)           # !
```

List Range Substitutions

Brush has a special form of list indexing which yields a list range rather than a single element. In this form, a colon is used to separate the start and end indices.

Conceptually, the indices refer not to the elements but rather to the spaces between them. The first index gives the space before the indicated element, and the second index gives the space after. The returned list range subtends all the elements between the selected spaces.

If the second index comes before the first, the range is empty; it refers only to the space preceding the first element. If the second index is omitted (but there is still a colon), it defaults to "-1". Since the second index refers to the space after the indicated element, "-1" corresponds to the space before the first element of the list. Consequently, omitting the second index always results in an empty range.

In range substitution, indexes before or after the end of the list are clamped to the list length.

```
set &data (a b c d e f g h)
: $data{0:end}        # a b c d e f g
: $data{0:0}          # a
: $data{-5:2}         # a b c
: $data{end:end}      # h
: $data{1:end-1}      # b c d e f g
: $data{end-4:4}      # d e
: $data{3:3}          # d
: $data{3:}           #
```

A list range substitution may not have any further indexes applied to it. This is because it does not refer to any one element of the variable; instead it constructs a new value.

Python has a similar feature, though it is called slices instead of ranges. Python end-relative indexing works differently than Tcl or Brush indexing.

Strided List Range Substitutions

The second index may be followed by another colon and a nonzero integer expression giving the stride. The default stride is "1", but this can be overridden to skip elements and/or reverse the list.

If the stride is negative, the before/after space convention is reversed, and the second index defaults to "end+1" if not explicitly specified. For negative stride, the first index denotes the space following the element, and the second index denotes the space preceding the element.

```
set &data (a b c d e f g h)
: $data(0:end:2}      # a c e g
: $data(1:end:2}      # b d f h
: $data{end:0:-1}     # h g f e d c b a
: $data{end:end:-1}   # h
: $data{end::-1}      #
: $data{end:0:-2}     # h f d b
: $data{end-1:0:-2}   # g e c a
```

A stride of "2" is useful for getting a list of all keys or values in a dictionary. "-1" stride provides an easy way to invert a dictionary such that its former values map back to its former keys.

Computed Variable Names

Tcl $-substitution only allows indirection inside array element names. The [set] command is required if the base variable name is computed, i.e. involves a substitution. Looked at another way, variable substitutions cannot be nested in Tcl.

Brush changes this by adding more variable name quoting styles. Tcl supports "$var" for literal names consisting of alphanumerics, underscores, and "::" namespace separators. Tcl also supports "${var}" for arbitrary literal names. Brush additionally supports "$"var"" wherein "var" can involve any kind of nested substitution.

A simple example would be one variable containing the name of another: "$"$x"". The value of variable "x" names the variable whose value is the overall result of the substitution. In Tcl, this can be done only by "[set $x]", short of [eval] and quoting hell[24].

"$"var"" notation nests. There is no ambiguity between the opening and closing double quotes since only the opening double quote has a leading dollar sign. I do not expect this to be needed often, but it exists for the sake of generality. For example, "$"$"xy"$z"" means:

1. Concatenate the values of variables "x" and "y" to get "xy".

2. Get the value of the variable named "xy", which is called "$"$x$y"".

3. Concatenate that value "$"$x$y"" with the value of variable "z" to get "$"$x$y"$z".

4. The result is the value of the variable named "$"$x$y"$z", called "$"$"xy"$z"".

Written in Tcl, this would be "[set [set xy]$z]"; swap "$"" for "[set " and """ for "]". This notation remains valid in Brush; it is just no longer required.

It is important to note that looking up variables with single-argument [set] precludes using the list and dictionary indexing described above. This is because element indexing is not a general-purpose operator operating on values, but rather is a directive to $-substitution operating on variables. (However, "$[set ...](index)" notation can be used; see below.)

Brush does *not* have a "$$var" notation, which presumably would be shorthand for "$"$var"". This is done to avoid ambiguity. Without the double quotes, it would not be clear whether any subsequent indexes apply to the nested variable substitution or the outer variable substitution. Would "$$foo(bar)" mean "$"$foo(bar)"" or "$"$foo"(bar)"?

```
set (&xyz &v1 &v2) (abc x z)
: $"${v1}y${v2}"     # abc
```

Functional Substitution

In many functional contexts, the value being indexed is not stored in a variable, but is returned by a command. [dict] and [list] can certainly be used to index such a value, but $-substitution is extended to make its compact notation directly usable even in the absence of a variable. The syntax is "$[script]", and the result of [script] is the value being indexed.

Functional substitution only makes sense in combination with indexing. "$[script]" with no indexing is equivalent to "[script]".

For example,

```
some_command            # a b c d e f g h
: $[some_command]       # a b c d e f g h
: $[some_command]{0:end:2}  # a c e g
: $[some_command](c)    # d
```

Be careful not to confuse "$[script]" with "$"[script]"", which is ordinary variable substitution where the variable name determined by script substitution.

Dereferencing

In addition to dictionary and list indexing, $-substitution supports one additional directive: the "@" dereference operator. The precise meaning of references will be discussed shortly.

In a $-substitution, "@"'s can follow the variable name and may be freely mixed with dictionary and list indexes. "@" takes the value in the variable (or element thereof), treats it as a reference, and tries to obtain the referenced value. Further indexing and dereferencing can follow "@" if the referenced value is a dictionary, list, or reference.

This example shows how to get a variable's value, given a reference to that variable:

```
set &x data             # data
set &ref &x             # &123
: $ref@                 # data
```

Dereferencing can be used repeatedly and in combination with other methods of indexing:

```
set &x (a 1 b 2)        # a 1 b 2
set &y (a 10 b 20)      # a 10 b 20
set &rx &x              # &123
set &ry &y              # &124
set &rrx &rx            # &125
set &rry &ry            # &126
set &rlist (&rrx &rry)  # &125 &126
: $rlist{1}             # &126
: $rlist{1}@            # &124
: $rlist{1}@@           # a 10 b 20
: $rlist{1}@@(b)        # 20
```

You may wish to revisit these examples after reading the section on references.

Substitution Syntax Comparison

The following table summarizes all the valid forms of substitution by comparing the Tcl and Brush notations side-by-side.

Substitution Type	Tcl	Brush
Simple name	`$simple_name`	`$simple_name`
Verbatim name	`${name_with_metachars}`	`${name_with_metachars}`
Computed name	`[set name_with_substitution]`	`$"name_with_substitution"`
Functional	`[script]`	`$[script]`
Single list index	`[lindex $name index]`	`$name{index}`
Multiple list index	`[lindex $name i1 i2 ...]`	`$name{i1 i2 ...}`
Pathed list index	`[lindex $name path]`	`$name{{*}path}`
List range	`[lrange $name first last]`	`$name{first:last}`
Empty list range	`[list]`	`$name{first:}`
Strided list range	Not Easily Available	`$name{first:last:stride}`
Empty strided list range	`[list]`	`$name{first::stride}`
Array index	`$simple_name(index)`	Not Available
Single dict index	`[dict get $name key]`	`$name(key)`
Explicit single dict index	`[dict get $name key]`	`$name((key))`
Multiple dict index	`[dict get $name k1 k2 ...]`	`$name(k1 k2 ...)`
Pathed dict index	`[dict get $name {*}path]`	`$name({*}path)`
Dereference	`[upvar 1 $name var; set var]`	`$name@`

Notes:

- "`simple_name`" is a string of one or more alphanumerics, underscores, or "`::`" namespace separators.

- "`name_with_metachars`" is a string consisting of any characters except closing brace.

- "`name_with_substitution`" is any sequence of characters on which the interpreter will perform variable, backslash, and script substitution to determine the variable name.

- "`$name`" is any valid `$`-substitution except for list ranging. This definition is recursive.

- Functional substitution is only useful in combination with indexing.

- Pathed and multiple list/dictionary indexing can be combined in a single operation.

- The Tcl dereference example is approximate. Many possible implementations exist.

References

Brush's powerful new $-substitution mechanism is only half of the equation. What good is reading a variable if it can't be written in the first place? To create or modify a variable or element, it is necessary to name it without taking its value, then to pass that name to [set].

In Tcl this is very simple: write the variable name, and it's done. Like everything else, a variable name is nothing more than a string.

I wanted to do the same in Brush, but I also wanted to be able to name elements in the same way as in $-substitution. Sadly, these goals conflict. Brush's variable and element names are not limited to simple literals but are an expression language which the interpreter does not always try to parse correctly. To correct this problem, Brush has a special reference syntax used for naming variables and elements.

Difficulties with Naming

Much like unbraced [expr], simply writing the variable name (no leading "$") has numerous problems when indexing is applied:

- *Syntax errors.* "matrix{2 3}" is actually parsed as two words since the interpreter splits the word on whitespace. Remember, a word is only brace-quoted if its *first character* is "{"[25].

- *Security holes.* "contacts($name)" can delete all your files if "$name" came from some untrustworthy source who maliciously set it to "[exec rm -rf ~]"[26].

- *Impaired performance.* With "data{$index}", there is no single Tcl_Obj in which it is possible to cache the parsed form of the variable name; string concatenation and parsing must be done every time.

- *Surprising results.* Put that first example in context: "[set matrix{2 3}]". This is actually legal Tcl. It means to set the value of variable "matrix{2" to "3}", which is surely not what was intended.

Tcl array variables are similarly afflicted, though to a much lesser degree. When preceded by "$" they work without issue; otherwise quoting is required when the key contains whitespace.

These issues arise due to the interpreter's lack of support for variable names when not performing substitution. Without "$", the interpreter treats a variable name like any other word, even though that means processing whitespace in a way that appears inconsistent with variable substitution.

---

25 http://www.tcl.tk/man/tcl8.6/TclCmd/Tcl.htm#M10 If the first character of a word is open brace ("{"), ...

26 http://xkcd.com/327/ Humorous but cautionary depiction of such an injection attack coming from an unlikely source. However, I disagree with the moral ("sanitize your inputs"), since it is a band-aid for a problem that can be fixed more efficiently and thoroughly by *never reparsing substitution results*.

What's more, the interpreter does its own substitution, as with any other word, then [set] reparses the substitution results, performing another round of substitution in the process. This opens up the same security hole experienced by [expr] when its arguments were already substituted by the interpreter.

Introducing References

The similarities with [expr] are instructive. Brush could adopt Tcl [expr]'s solution and strongly recommend that the user brace-quote any variable names. However, this would likely lead to another problem experienced by Tcl [expr]: Because the consequences are not immediately apparent, programmers forget to use braces. Worse, substitutions embedded within names will not always be performed at the right times or in the right stack frames.

Taking a cue from its own solution to the [expr] problem, Brush instead defines a streamlined notation for declaring that a word is a variable name. The interpreter knows how to handle variable substitutions, so it is more than adequately equipped to handle variable names. All that is needed is a hint from the programmer to enable variable name mode. The interpreter, seeing this hint, knows that the word is a *value* that names a variable or an element thereof. Such a value is called a reference.

Brush prefixes a word with an "&" ampersand to indicate that it is a reference. "&" is chosen for this purpose because C++ already associates that symbol with the term "reference." This behaves like a quoting mechanism in several ways:

- It tells the interpreter to apply parenthesis matching and other variable naming rules, rather than merely looking for the next whitespace, to identify the word boundary.

- Only a whole word can be a reference, and the first character of the word ("&" in this case) determines how that word is treated.

- The output word, a.k.a. the value or the string representation, is not necessarily identical to the literal text of the script.

&-references support indexing, same as for $-substitution. The notation is obtained simply by writing "&" instead of "$", though "&" only has special meaning as the word's first character.

Brush forbids the use of a "bare" string where a variable reference is expected. This is done for consistency and to avoid the problems described in the previous section. To convert a variable name (itself contained in a variable) to a reference, simply use "&"$name"". As mentioned in the section on substitution with computed variable names, the double quotes are required to avoid ambiguous cases.

Since a reference is a value, it can be returned; passed as an argument; or stored in a variable, list, or dictionary. References do not always have to be typed literally; they can be the product of substitution. Whereas Tcl requires [upvar] or [uplevel] to access the caller's variables, in Brush they can be reached simply by using a reference passed from the caller.

Unlike C++ references, Brush references must be created explicitly, like C pointers.

Value of a Reference

A reference's value is "**&**" followed by the referent variable's interpreter-wide unique ID. If the reference has any indexing, it follows the ID using the same notation used in the script, albeit with embedded substitutions already performed.

References are strings, but that is not all they are. Let's compare references to Tcl I/O channels to illustrate by analogy.

In Tcl, an I/O channel is a string, e.g. "`file5`", but it is also a key in a hash table mapping to the internal data structure that actually implements the channel. Likewise, references index into an interpreter-wide variable table, e.g. "`&123`" for variable #123.

Tcl I/O channels are created using the [`open`] command which does two things: create the internal structures, and generate a unique string which maps to said structures. Similarly, when Brush executes a command line containing an **&**-reference, it creates a variable and an associated reference value.

Not all references are given unique values. If multiple references within a single stack frame refer to the same-named variable, the interpreter gives them all the same value, assuming they have the same element indexing. Contrast with Tcl I/O channels, where opening one file multiple times yields distinct channels.

Early and Late Binding

At the moment a reference is created, all embedded substitutions are immediately performed. In this way, references capture a snapshot of the interpreter state. At the time the reference is created, it decides forever which variable or elements thereof are being referenced. This is early binding.

In this example, a reference to a variable's list element is created. Two methods are used to make the reference, but the same reference, with the same index, is obtained each time. "`&r1`" uses direct substitution, whereas "`&r2`" uses the "`@`" dereference operator on a reference to the index variable. Because of early binding, changing the index variable after creating the references does not affect them.

```
set (&x &i &j) ((a b c) 1 &i)
set &r1 &x{$i}    # &123(1)
set &r2 &x{$j@}   # &123(1)
: ($r1@ $r2@)     # b b
set &i 2
: ($r1@ $r2@)     # b b
```

A reference can contain late-bound indexes which are not decided until it is dereferenced. This is done by using the "`^`" late-binding dereference operator when constructing the reference. This operator causes a normal "`@`" dereference operator to be placed in the reference value, and the "`@`" will not be processed until the reference itself is dereferenced.

Modifying the previous example to use "^" instead of "@" or bare "$" causes $r1 and $r2 to contain embedded references with "@"s to be applied at dereference time. This defers indexing, so changing the value of $i does have an effect. Notice that $r1 and $r2 each contain references to not only the "x" variable but also the "i" variable.

```
set (&x &i) ((a b c) 1)
set &j &i          # &124
set &r1 &x{&i^}    # &123(&124@)
set &r2 &x{$j^}    # &123(&124@)
: ($r1@ $r2@)      # b b
set &i 2
: ($r1@ $r2@)      # c c
```

Late binding can only be applied to indexes, not to the variable name. This restriction is necessary because the referenced variable must be clearly identified in order for garbage collection to work. If an existing reference value could be coerced to reference any variable, no variables could ever be finalized.

The "^" late binding operator is only recognized when constructing a reference, and even then only inside list and dictionary indexing. In every other context, it has no special meaning.

Building References from References

Given a reference stored in a variable "$ref", the value of the referent variable (or element) is obtained by "$ref@". To make a new reference to an element of that result, the notation is "&$ref@" followed by the additional indexing operators, for example "&$ref@{$i}".

To understand this, start with "&name{$i}" and recognize that "name" can be computed. Now use "$ref@" in place of "name" to get "&$ref@{$i}". This works even if "$ref" already contains element indexing or dereference operators. Such a thing is called an additive reference.

You may recall that $-substitution does not support "$$name", only "$"$name"". Therefore this "&$ref@" notation is an exception to the rule that references are constructed by writing the substitution that would yield the desired element, only with "&" instead of "$" up front.

Another way of looking at it is that the entire substitution (everything but the leading "&") is performed, though not to get the value, but rather to locate the element to which the reference will point.

```
set &var (a (1 2 3) b (4 5 6))
set &ref1 &var          # &123
set &ref2 &var(b)       # &123(b)
set &ref3 &$ref1@(b)    # &123(b)
set &ref4 &$ref2@{1}    # &123(b){1}
: $ref3@                # 4 5 6
: $ref3@{1}             # 5
: $ref4@                # 5
```

Just like with normal references, the "^" late-binding dereference can be used in the index components of an additive reference. It will be replaced with an "@" dereference operator in the output reference value.

```
set &var (a (1 2 3) b (4 5 6))
set (&k &i) (b 1)
set &ref1 &var(&k^)       # &123(&124@)
set &ref2 &$ref1@{&i^}    # &123(&124@){&125@}
: $ref2@                  # 5
set (&k &i) (a 2)
: $ref2@                  # 3
```

"&$name" is illegal because references point to variables or elements, not anonymous values, and "$name" yields a value. However, "&"$name"" is valid for creating a reference given a variable *name*.

The [ref link] command, described later, provides another way to create additive references.

The inverse operation, removing indexing from an existing reference, is not defined at this time. A [ref] command ensemble could facilitate reference examination and manipulation.

Three Stages of Reference Processing

Compilation. When a script containing &-references is submitted to the interpreter for compilation, the &-references are transformed into bytecodes that will produce a reference value upon execution. The bytecodes may use substitution and concatenation to determine the variable name and/or the indexing. Nesting and dereferencing may also be employed.

Execution. Given the bytecodes emitted by the compiler, the bytecode execution engine makes a reference value. The engine checks if the reference names a variable already present in the local stack frame. If not, a new variable is created in the global variable table, and its name and ID are put in the local stack frame. The reference value consists of the variable ID and any indexing instructions.

Dereferencing. When the reference value is given to a C function that needs to access the variable, it passes the reference Tcl_Obj to functions that read, modify, or unset the variable or an element of its value. This can be done immediately after the reference is created, or it can happen some time later, maybe even after the variable's stack frame has exited.

References and [set]

As shown by examples throughout this paper, &-references are used as the first argument to [set] in order to create variables or modify their values. Naturally, [set] supports not only simple references to variables, but also references to variable elements. In this way, [set] can be used in place of Tcl's [lset] or [dict set].

```
set &x (a 1 b 2)     # a 1 b 2
set &x(a) 0; : $x    # a 0 b 2
set &x(c) 4; : $x    # a 0 b 2 c 4
set &x{1} 1; : $x    # a 1 b 2 c 4
```

As "&x(c)" shows in the above example, references can be constructed to nonexistent elements. [set]'ing them creates the element. This mirrors how variables are created initially: the reference exists *before* the variable is made.

Creating list elements is limited by the requirement that the index numbering have no gaps. Only indices "0" through "end+1" can be assigned. When assigning to "end+1" (or the equivalent absolute index), the element is appended to the list, so [lappend] is not needed.

```
set &x{end+1} a; : $x        # a
set &x{end+1} b; : $x        # a b
set &x{2} c     ; : $x        # a b c
```

Assigning to list ranges works like [lreplace]: the indicated range is replaced with the new value, which is treated as a list of elements. [linsert]'s behavior is made possible by assigning to zero-width ranges; the empty range is "replaced" with the new list. Empty ranges are constructed when the second element comes before the first, which is the default when a colon is used with no second index.

```
set &x (a b c)
set &x{0:} _          ; : $x    # _ a b c
set &x{1:} (1 2)      ; : $x    # _ 1 2 a b c
set &x{3:4} ()        ; : $x    # _ 1 2 c
set &x{end:} ((x y)); : $x    # _ 1 2 {x y} c
set &x{end+1:} z      ; : $x    # _ 1 2 {x y} c z
```

When the list range has a negative stride, the inserted element order is reversed.

```
set &x{0::-1} (a b c) ; : $x # c b a
set &x{1:2:-1} (x y z); : $x # c z y x
set &x{end::-1} (1 2) ; : $x # c z y x 2 1
set &x{-1::-1} (3 4)  ; : $x # 4 3 c z y x 2 1
```

Be cautious of negative stride. An above example shows that assigning to "&x{end:}" puts elements *before* the current last element, which may seem surprising but is consistent with non-range list indexing. Negative stride reverses the before/after space convention, so "&x{end::-1}" references the space *after* the last element, and "&x{-1::-1}" references the space *before* the first element.

Assigning to a range with non-unit stride is tricky. The concept is that only the elements included in the range are replaced with new elements. For the sake of sanity, Brush requires the replacement list to be empty or to have the same element count as the range.

```
set &x (a 1 b 2)              # a 1 b 2
set &x{0:end:2} (A B) ; : $x # A 1 B 2
set &x{end:0:-2} (3 4); : $x # A 4 B 3
set &x{0:end:2} ()    ; : $x # 4 3
```

References and [unset]

In Tcl, variables are created by [set]. Brush is slightly different; variables are created by &-reference constructors, and [set] gives them their initial value.

[unset], likewise, works a little differently. Tcl's [unset] destroys the variable, and it is no longer accessible. Brush's [unset] removes the variable's value, as if [set] had never been called. [unset] does not remove the variable name from the local stack frame, so newly created references to the same-named variable will have the same value as existing references.

After being [unset], the variable can be given a value again by passing its reference to [set]. So long as it has extant references, the variable remains in the interpreter's variable table, even though it might not always have a value. All references continue to point to the same variable; [unset] does not break this link. In this way, an unset variable (or reference thereto) can be used as a "null" distinct from empty string.

[unset] works not only with references to variables, but also references to elements of variables. [unset]'ing an element means to remove it, so [unset] obsoletes [dict unset] and zero-element [lreplace].

Applying [unset] to a list index removes the element, causing higher-indexed elements to be shifted down one slot. [unset] on list ranges behaves similarly. For strided list ranges, the indicated elements are all removed as if they had been [unset] one-by-one.

```
set &x (a b c d e f g)         # a b c d e f g
unset &x{0}           ; : $x # b c d e f g
unset &x{end-1:end}   ; : $x # b c d e
unset &x{1:end:2}     ; : $x # b d
unset &x(b)           ; : $x #
unset &x              ; : $x # can't read "x": variable is unset
```

It's instructive to look at the error messages caused by unset variables.

```
: $z      # can't read "z": no such variable
: &z      # &123
: $z      # can't read "z": variable is unset
set &z    # can't dereference "&123": variable is unset
```

1. The first line attempts $-substitution on a never-before-seen variable, so the error says "no such variable."

2. Next, a reference is created, though its value is not saved anywhere. The variable's reference count is momentarily two, then it drops to one when the result is ignored. The remaining reference is from the local stack frame which now maps "z" to "&123".

3. The third line again tries to get the value, but this time the variable reference is found in the local stack frame. However, the substitution still fails because the variable has never been given a value.

4. Last, $-substitution is eschewed in favor of single-argument [set]. Like "$", [set] sees that the variable has no value. Unlike "$", the error message does not contain the variable name. This is because [set]'s argument is a reference value "&123", which does not embed a variable name.

Using [ref link] to Link Variables to References

The new [ref link] command links a referent variable or element into the local stack frame. The result appears to work like a local variable, but all accesses to it forward to the original variable. Similarly, any attempts to create references to this new linked variable actually end up creating references to the original variable.

[ref link] takes two arguments: the existing reference and the new variable *name*. It is important to stress that the second argument is a name, *not* a reference. This is not so unusual; recall that [proc]'s second argument is also a list of names, not references.

```
ref link &old new
: &old              # &123
: &new              # &123
ref link &old(x) elem
: &elem(y z)        # &123(x y z)
```

[ref link] takes the place of [upvar]. Unlike [upvar], [ref link] has no need of a stack frame level argument. This is because all variables are effectively global; it is their *names* that are only recognized locally.

Brush retains [upvar] for symmetry with [uplevel] which is still required.

If more than two arguments are passed to [ref link], they are used as additional reference/variable name pairs, in the same manner as [upvar].

If [ref link] is given the name of an existing variable, the variable name is retargeted to the new reference, decrementing the reference count of the old variable, likely triggering its finalization. If the reference argument is empty string, the variable name is simply removed from the local stack frame.

[ref link] may be part of a larger [ref] ensemble featuring commands to examine and manipulate references.

Comparison with Tcl

Despite not being formally recognized by the interpreter, Tcl has references too; they are simply variable names. Names are values that can be passed around and used in stack frames other than the one in which they were created. However, for them to be used elsewhere, the relative or absolute stack frame must be known, e.g. "this is my caller's variable" or "this is a global variable", and then [upvar] or [global] can link the variable into the local stack frame.

In addition to the requirement that the stack level be passed around out-of-band, the referenced variable cannot outlive its stack frame. If this is a problem, the variable must be created globally, perhaps in a namespace.

This leads to a new problem: the variable's lifetime becomes indefinite, and the script must be careful to finalize it when it is no longer conceptually reachable. Also, the script is responsible for generating unique names for the global variables.

Tcl "references" can only name variables, not elements. (Tcl arrays are collections of variables, not values.) An element reference scheme could be devised, but it would have to be implemented using custom accessor commands; basic $-substitution would be unavailable, short of elaborate variable traces.

Brush's references eliminate the need for [upvar] and [global] in the case of commands accepting variable references (names) as arguments. The identity of the originating stack frame is irrelevant because references are indexes into an interpreter-wide variable table.

Brush retains [upvar] and [global] unmodified, plus it adds a [ref link] command to link a local variable to any variable or element thereof given its reference.

Since Brush variables are kept in a global table, they can survive their stack frame for as long as they are reachable through references. This makes it easier to create anonymous mutable data objects accessible only to parts of the code which have been given the reference.

Brush references can name elements as well as entire variables, and indexed and unindexed references can be used interchangeably. This design largely obsoletes Tcl arrays, which are collections of variables that can be managed individually or as a group.

Brush retains Tcl's variable traces, though it loses out on array traces. An alternative to array traces may yet be defined, but it would face difficulties due to the element traces being on values rather than entire variables.

Reference Syntax Summary

The same notes apply to this table as for the substitution syntax summary.

Reference Type	Syntax
Simple name	`&simple_name`
Verbatim name	`&{name_with_metachars}`
Computed name	`&"name_with_substitution"`
Additive	`&$name@`
Single list index	`&name{index}`
Multiple list index	`&name{i1 i2 ...}`
Pathed list index	`&name{{*}path}`
List range	`&name{first:last}`
Empty list range	`&name{first:}`
Strided list range	`&name{first:last:stride}`
Empty strided list range	`&name{first::stride}`
Single dict index	`&name(key)`
Explicit single dict index	`&name((key))`
Multiple dict index	`&name(k1 k2 ...)`
Pathed dict index	`&name({*}path)`
Early-binding dereference	`&name{$name2@}` or `$name($name2@)`
Late-binding dereference	`&name{$name2^}` or `$name($name2^)`

Garbage Collection

Garbage collection in Brush is only preliminarily specified. It is a work in progress, and I enthusiastically invite suggestions to refine or replace the scheme defined here.

Tcl I/O channels must be explicitly destroyed using the [chan close] command. This is very different from Brush references (actually, variables), which are garbage-collected. When a Brush reference value's refcount[27] drops below one, it is finalized, and its referent variable's reference count is decremented, triggering cascading destruction whenever the value or variable does not have multiple referrers.

This simple scheme is defeated by circular references which prevent otherwise unreachable variables from ever being cleaned up. I am not well-versed in advanced garbage collection algorithms, but Frédéric Bonnet's Colibri[28] implements an exact, generational, copying, mark-and-sweep, garbage collector, so perhaps Colibri can be used to store values in Brush.

References and Shimmering

Reference tracking challenges EIAS semantics. If a reference shimmers away from its reference internal representation, despite keeping the same string representation, should the referent variable's refcount be decremented? Answering "yes" breaks EIAS, but handling this corner case will be costly.

One possible solution is to not decrement when the value is not actually changing, merely shimmering, but that leads to another question: when should the variable's refcount eventually be decremented?

In order to check if a value object contains references, it is necessary to *attempt* to convert it to a reference or list of references. Clearly, this is an expensive operation which should be done as infrequently as possible:

- This check is only done when the value is being destroyed.

- Type conversion is only attempted if the value is flagged as possibly being a reference.

- If the value's internal representation is a list, its contents are recursively scanned to find flagged values or nested lists. (Remember, a dictionary is a list.)

Value objects with internal type of reference, such as those generated by an &-reference constructor, have their reference flag set, as do any values made by concatenating a flagged value. Lists and dictionaries containing flagged values are *not* themselves flagged, at least not until they shimmer to pure string, at which point their values are made via concatenation with flagged values. Shimmering back to list or dictionary clears the flag, since it is transferred to any of the contained values which fit the reference schema.

---

27 http://www.tcl.tk/man/tcl8.6/TclLib/Object.htm Official documentation of Tcl_Objs and their refcounts.
   http://wiki.tcl.tk/tcl_obj+refcount+howto Description of how to properly manage Tcl_Obj refcounts in C code.
28 http://wiki.tcl.tk/colibri Colibri is the string and data type infrastructure implemented by FB for Cloverfield.

Unshared string values can be modified in-place, possibly adding or removing a reference in the process. (This is not typical usage; the list and dictionary commands are preferred, and they have no need of flags since their elements are distinct values.) When C code modifies a string value in such a way that could add or remove a reference, it must call a function to check the modified string or substring for references and to update the flag accordingly.

Regarding "reference or list of references": This phrase interacts badly with EIAS. It collides with a limitation of duck typing, being that the interpreter only knows the type of a value when the script tells it the type. Here, the interpreter is forced to guess types. Its algorithm is as follows:

1. A value is a reference if it has reference internal type or can be converted to one.

2. Else, if a value has list (which includes dictionary) internal type or can be converted to a list with length *not equal to one*, it is a list. In this case, recursively apply this algorithm to each element.

Circular References

The scheme described above is vulnerable to circular references, e.g. [set &x &x]. Since its value refers to itself, the "x" variable's reference count will never drop below one and will never be destroyed. Flushing out circular references requires expensive reachability analysis.

When a stack frame is destroyed, the refcounts of all its variables are decremented. The frame's surviving variables are checked for reachability from any active stack frames, including those of all coroutines, within the current interpreter. This test is also done when a variable is removed from the stack frame using [ref link] but it still has positive refcount.

The reachability search is performed in an order designed to check the most likely places first:

1. Current stack frame, in the [ref link] case.

2. Late stack frame's returned value, in the [return] case.

3. Global stack frame, including all namespaces.

4. Current coroutine's stack frames, if in a coroutine.

5. Main routine stack frames.

6. All inactive coroutine stack frames.

7. Additional object stores registered by extensions with data "outside" of the interpreter.

Any variables found to be unreachable are destroyed. Reachability is defined as being referenced by a value object within, or reachable from, a stack frame. Only values flagged as possibly containing references are checked for references. The process of checking causes shimmering to reference or list.

The reachability search may be optimized by maintaining an interpreter-wide list of value objects contained within any of the searched stack frames.

Performance

The foregoing may sound extremely expensive, but it is made necessary by two corner cases:

- References embedded in strings that *could* be lists.
- Circular references.

I expect these cases to be rare in practice, so I designed this preliminary garbage collection algorithm to minimize cost in common cases.

If the script avoids shimmering away from reference or list-of-references, the only reference-flagged objects will in fact have internal type of reference, and the interpreter will never try to shimmer values back to reference or list-of-references.

[proc] bodies legitimately using circular references can significantly improve performance by breaking the reference prior to using [ref link] or [return].

Circular reference reachability analysis is only done when variables outlive their stack frames or survive [ref link]. This happens when a procedure returns a reference to a local variable, or if it puts a local reference inside a [proc] or other such object. The variable lives on, but after being separated from its stack frame, it can only be accessed via pre-made references.

In the course of shimmering a reference-flagged value to list, its reference flag is cleared, so the shimmering is a one-time thing. Basically the interpreter allows the script to shimmer from reference or list-of-references, but it forces the type back when the value is being destroyed or a reachability analysis is being done. Due to EIAS, this shimmering does *not* result in any values being changed, and the only cost of shimmering is CPU time.

Alternatives

As mentioned above, Colibri may provide some solutions, and it may be directly usable by Brush. I have not delved into its implementation to see precisely how it works.

Jim references[29] track values, not variables. Values persist so long as references to them exist, and references are values. Brush's design depends on references naming variables rather than values, so this is a fundamental difference.

Jim does not attempt to clean up circular references. Brush could adopt this as a design constraint, since Jim is successful despite this limitation.

Jim scans all existing value objects, including those not reachable from any stack frame, for the sake of simplicity and to avoid prematurely destroying references contained only "inside" an extension not fully exposed to the interpreter. Brush could do the same, at the expense of not being able to detect circular references.

Jim skips values that are not pure strings because they cannot be references. However, this assumption is invalidated by regular expressions and possibly other types. This limitation

---

29   http://wiki.tcl.tk/jim Jim is a small-footprint reimplementation of Tcl with some advanced features.
     http://wiki.tcl.tk/jim+references Description, demonstration, and discussion of the Jim references system.

may be acceptable because there is no legitimate reason for a script to treat a value as both a reference and a regular expression.

Jim is documented to skip strings that are not exactly references, e.g. they have the wrong string length (Jim references are always 42 characters long, for performance and cosmic reasons.) This does not match the current implementation: Jim checks all pure strings to see if they contain substrings that are valid references. This is done to handle the case of reference lists shimmering to string. Brush probably can't do the same, since Brush references are harder to detect than Jim references.

Command Dispatch

To support its functional programming goal, Brush redefines command dispatch in a way that makes commands be values. A variable containing a command value is directly executable, or an anonymous command value can be invoked. Since command values are stored in variables, they enjoy the scoping and lifetime rules of variables, plus they can be passed around by value or reference as well as by name, or can be put inside data structures.

This design eliminates the value/command dichotomy[30] present since Tcl's inception. Tcl's [apply] command does this as well, but it must be used explicitly. Brush makes it automatic, plus it opens the door for more types of commands.

Unlike Tcl, Brush command and variable names can collide; they compete for the same "namespace". This is a drawback for some scripts that use a variable named the same as a proc to store the proc's static data[31]. However, as will be discussed later, it is possible to instead keep the data inside the proc itself, persisting from one invocation to the next.

$-substitution is implied for the first word of each command. This has two consequences. One, a command name is actually the name of a variable containing the command. Two, the command name can use any of the indexing notations valid for $-substitution. If the command is named via explicit $-substitution, the automatic $-substitution is inhibited.

When a command is invoked, the local stack frame is searched, just like ordinary $-substitution. If that search fails, the local stack's home namespace is searched, then the global namespace "::". As a last resort, the interpreter's [unknown] command is called.

The value of a command is a list. The first element of this list is the command type, and subsequent elements vary from type to type. The command type word is not the name of a command; it is handled internally by the bytecode compiler and/or execution engine. It is possible for a command to have the same name as a command type.

In addition to the string/list representation, command values have an internal representation containing executable bytecodes and/or type-specific configuration data. Beware that

---

30 http://wiki.tcl.tk/getting+rid+of+the+value/command+dichotomy+for+tcl+9 Commands are not first-class objects.
31 http://wiki.tcl.tk/gadgets Gadgets are objects with code in a proc and data in a variable, both named the same.

performing list commands (even ostensibly read-only list indexing, such as "$cmd{$i}") will cause the command value to shimmer away from its compiled command representation. This does not impact program correctness but does force a time-consuming recompilation. Nevertheless, it may be useful within debug contexts or for very dynamic coding techniques.

Each command type can have an associated finalizer routine which cleans up any exterior resources and data structures associated with the command.

One major difficulty for introspection and error message generation is that command values are anonymous. They only borrow the name of their container variable, but that does not help in situations where the command value is substituted and/or computed on the spot.

Lambda Commands

A lambda[32] is an anonymous proc. Its value is a list with three or four elements:

1. The word "lambda". This distinguishes between lambdas and other command types.

2. Formal argument list, which can include required, optional, defaulted, catchall, and bound arguments.

3. Script body. This will be executed in a new stack frame initially containing one variable for each formal argument.

4. Namespace *(optional)*. When the script invokes a command or calls [variable] to link a variable into the local stack frame, this namespace is searched before looking in the global "::" namespace. By default, the namespace is computed from the command name (if the command is global) or inherited from the local stack frame (if local).

A Tcl-like [proc] command can be implemented simply:

```
set &::proc (lambda (nameref arglist body) {
    set $nameref (lambda $arglist $body); :
})
```

This creates a lambda and binds it to the name [proc] in the global namespace "::". When [proc] is later executed, it constructs a lambda from its arguments and binds it to the variable indicated by its first argument.

Bound arguments can be used to capture the procedure's creation-time environment. If the bound arguments are set to references[33], and the same references are given to other procs, the procs will be able to share some variables, thereby establishing an object system. The references can be to variables local to the stack frame that created the procs, so they will be anonymous and inaccessible outside of the constructor procedure, and they will be finalized when the procs are destroyed.

---

32 http://wiki.tcl.tk/lambda Lambdas are anonymous functions, or procs in the Tcl/Brush parlance.

33 http://wiki.tcl.tk/closures Brush implements closures by allowing the programmer to bind arguments to references to variables local to the stack frame in which the proc is being created.

Reference-bound arguments can be turned into local variables using the [ref link] command to replace the argument variable with the referent variable. This avoids the constant need for the "@" dereference operator.

To demonstrate, here is a solution for Paul Graham's accumulator generator problem[34]. For the sake of example, this implementation deviates from Paul Graham's rules by offering defaults for $value and $increment.

```
proc &accum_gen ((val? 0)) {
    : (lambda ((valref= &val) (inc? 0)) {
        set $valref $($valref@ + inc)
    })
}
```

[accum_gen] takes an initial value argument from which it constructs a lambda that returns the sum of the initial value and its $inc argument. A reference to the initial value is bound to the lambda's $valref argument, so the lambda has sole access to a variable whose lifetime matches that of the lambda itself. The lambda, when executed, gets the value stored in that variable, adds $inc to it, stores the result into the variable, and returns said result.

```
set &accums (a [accum_gen 12] b [accum_gen 4])
accums(a) 0        # 12
accums(a) 5        # 17
accums(a) -2.5     # 14.5
accums(b) 6        # 10
```

Native Commands

Obviously, not all commands can be implemented in script; there must be a basis implemented in C. Native commands are commands written in C, etc. and compiled to machine code. Their implementation is opaque to the script, instead replaced by a numeric identifier. The value of a native command is a two- or three-element list:

1. The first word, "native", is the command type.

2. Numeric identifier for the command. This is *not* a pointer to the function; it is an index into the interpreter's native command table. This is done to prevent safe interpreters from calling unauthorized commands.

3. Namespace *(optional)*. This is only necessary if the command accesses namespace variables, which is vanishingly rare for native commands. If omitted, the namespace is determined in the same way as for lambdas.

In this example, [set] and [:] are revealed to be the 7th and 9th commands:

```
: $set          # native 7
: ${:}          # native 9
```

---

34 http://wiki.tcl.tk/accumulator+generator The challenge is to make a function that returns a function which returns the sum of all values ever passed to it. The accumulator's initial value is specified when the function is generated.

Curried Commands

Brush allows any command to be curried[35], meaning that one or more initial arguments are bound in advance. For example, a command that adds two numbers could be curried to make the first number always be "1", resulting in a command that increments a number.

A curried command's value is a list with at least two elements:

1. The word "curry" gives the command type tag.

2. Value of the command being curried, e.g. "native 74" or "lambda {x y} {: $(x+y)}". Since curried commands are commands, they can be nested.

3. Subsequent arguments serve as initial arguments to the command. A more efficient way to further curry a curried command is to append argument elements to its value.

The value of the above increment example is "curry {lambda {x y} {: $(x+y)}} 1", and it is constructed in a very simple and natural way:

```
proc &sum (x y) {: $(x+y)}
set &inc (curry $sum 1)    # curry {lambda {x y} {: $(x+y)}} 1
inc 5                       # 6
```

Prefix Commands

A prefix command is perhaps better termed a "command prefix[36] command"; it is a command value containing a command prefix. Since command prefixes are themselves commands, maybe the name could be "command command", except that's too confusing.

Prefix commands are almost identical to curry commands, except that the second list element is a command name instead of a command value.

```
proc &sum (x y) {: $(x+y)}
set &inc (prefix sum 1)     # prefix sum 1
inc 5                        # 6
```

Prefix commands are useful in situations where a command value is expected but you have only a command name. In that sense, it is the complement of the [apply] command, which enables execution of a lambda (which Brush generalizes to a command value) in contexts where a command prefix is expected.

Because the indicated command can be modified after the prefix command value is created, late binding can be implemented using prefix commands

Channel Commands

Tcl's I/O channels are represented in the interpreter by strings such as "stdout", "file5", or "sock304". They are constructed using [open], [socket], [chan create], [chan pipe], or extension commands, and they must be explicitly finalized using the [chan close] command.

---

35 http://wiki.tcl.tk/curry Curried functions accept arguments one at a time using nested single-argument functions.

36 http://wiki.tcl.tk/command+prefix A command prefix is a list containing a command name and some or all of its arguments, with the expectation that zero or more arguments will be appended and the result will be evaluated.

Brush I/O channels are constructed in the same way but are channel-type command values. This gives them several very interesting properties:

- Brush I/O channels function as command ensembles, so the [chan] command is unnecessary except for [chan names], [chan create], and [chan pipe].

- Values, including command values, are garbage collected. The finalizer for channel command values closes the channel. This makes explicit [chan close] optional, and [unset] can be used in its place. Additionally, garbage collection minimizes the need for [chan names].

The value of a channel is a list, and it is exceptionally simple:

1. The word "chan".

2. Name of the channel, same as in Tcl. For example, "stdout", "file5", or "sock304".

Global variables called $stdin, $stdout, and $stderr are pre-created, containing the values "chan stdin", "chan stdout", and "chan stderr", respectively. These variables work like commands (or objects, if you prefer), and they have subcommands à la [chan].

Here are some examples demonstrating a few usage possibilities:

```
stdout puts >>[stdin gets]<<    # copy from stdin to stdout, adding >> and <<
set &data [[open file] read]    # file is automatically closed after the read
set &out $stdout                # let stdout be accessed throughh another name
unset &out &stdout              # now both must be unset to close stdout
```

Interpreter, Coroutine, and Namespace Commands

Interpreters, coroutines, and namespaces are given the same treatment as channels; Brush promotes them all to be command values.

Ensemble Commands

Brush splits ensembles from namespaces because they can now be implemented directly inside a single value. Aside from the invocation, there is not much difference between an ensemble and a dictionary of command values,.

For demonstration purposes, here is a dictionary of command values. In this example, the keys are two-element lists, which is why the indexing is done using double parentheses: The inner pair is used to construct a list to be used as the key.

```
set &cmds ((msg 1) (lambda () (: hello))
          (msg 2) (lambda () (: goodbye)))
cmds((msg 1))                  # hello
cmds((msg 2))                  # goodbye
```

An ensemble command's value contains such a dictionary of command values, but it adds some configuration options. It is formatted as a two- or three-element list:

1. The word "ensemble".

2. Command dictionary mapping from subcommand names to command values. The keys are treated as lists to implement multiple-word subcommand names. It is an error for one key to equal or be a prefix of another key.

3. Configuration dictionary *(optional)*. If omitted, it is treated as if it were empty.

The configuration dictionary supports a subset of Tcl's [namespace ensemble] options[37]:

- "parameters": If present, the length of this list is the number of actual arguments accepted *between* the ensemble name and the subcommand name. Normally all arguments are expected to *follow* the subcommand name. The list elements are used as formal argument names to be displayed in error messages.

- "prefixes": If omitted or logically false, subcommand names must exactly match the keys in the command dictionary. If logically true, subcommand names can be any unambiguous prefix of the command dictionary keys.

- "unknown": If present and non-empty, contains a command value to be invoked whenever an unrecognized subcommand is called. The arguments to this command are the fully-qualified ensemble command name (if known, else empty string) and all its arguments, including the subcommand name(s). A prefix command may be useful here to use an existing command as the unknown handler, or the unknown handler can be specified inline and remain anonymous.

A command named [ensemble] may be defined to facilitate and optimize creating, querying, and reconfiguring ensemble command values. While ensembles can be managed using list and dictionary access, they have the side effect of shimmering away the ensemble command value's internal compiled representation.

Here is the previous example rewritten to use an ensemble command:

```
set &lookup (ensemble ((msg 1) (lambda () (: hello))
                       (msg 2) (lambda () (: goodbye))))
lookup msg 1         # hello
lookup msg 2         # goodbye
```

Object Commands

I have minimal experience with TclOO[38], but it seems likely an OO system can be built on top of Brush's command value mechanism. In the section on lambda commands, this paper already outlined ways to exploit references to share data between procs, such that the procs

---

37 http://www.tcl.tk/man/tcl8.6/TclCmd/namespace.htm#M34 Official documentation for ensemble options.

38 http://wiki.tcl.tk/tcloo TclOO is the first dedicated object-oriented system included in the official Tcl distribution.

together form an object with hidden data. The ensemble command system can further be used to neatly group those procs within a single object command value.

Object systems typically do more than just group code and data. They may offer inheritance, delegation, standardized interfaces, polymorphism, run-time type identification, and programmable finalization. To that end, Brush proposes (but does not yet specify) to adapt TclOO or a similar OO mechanism to an object command value.

Being able to customize finalization is the main reason why command values need to be a distinct command type. As already shown for channel commands, at the C level the command type registration system provides hooks for supplying a type-specific finalization routine. An object system would expose that hook at the script level, making it possible to script object cleanup.

Extension and Reflected Commands

Extensions can add custom command types. For example, Brush/Tk[39] may define window, image, and font command value types.

It may be useful to reflect this extension capability back into the script level so that new command types can be defined programmatically. In this way, fully custom object systems can be defined.

Conclusion

Brush offers an exciting palette of functionality designed to encourage programmer creativity and expression to blossom, as well as to attract new attention to the Tcl universe.

Everything in Brush is founded on the simple-yet-powerful Tcl **EIAS** philosophy. Within the framework of EIAS, Brush defines new reference and command values and integrates them with the interpreter, plus it unifies dictionaries and lists to optimize interchangeability.

Building upon Tcl, Brush streamlines and enhances the syntax to **encourage best practices** proven by long experience to promote efficiency and safety. The syntax improvements also make Brush more familiar to users of other programming languages.

References are exploited to establish a potent and compact **data structure access** notation through which even deeply nested, mixed data structures are easy to manipulate with minimal need for accessor commands.

Elegant **functional programming paradigms** arise from Brush's reference and command value design. References provide excellent control over variable access and lifetime, and command values are first-class citizens within the interpreter, fully exposed to the same powerful data manipulation infrastructure as any other kind of value.

---

39 http://wiki.tcl.tk/tk Tk is the most popular GUI toolkit used with Tcl.
    http://wiki.tcl.tk/gnocl Gnocl is an alternative GUI toolkit for Tcl that binds to Gtk+.

Tcl 2012
Chicago, IL
November 14-16, 2012

Session 6
November 15 15:15-16:15

editTableA Generic Display and Edit Widget for Database Applications

Clif Flynt
Noumena Corporation,
8888 Black Pine Ln,
Whitmore Lake, MI 48189,
http://www.noucorp.com
clif at noucorp dot com

October 24, 2012

Abstract

An application that includes a database always requires a set of pages to edit the contents of the database.

The bulk of the edit pages are simple and easy to write. Even with Tk's ease in constructing simple data-entry pagespages, writing a dozen procedures takes time that could be spent on the more interesting parts of a project.

The goal of the EditTables package is to provide a set of good enough pages with no effort on the part of the programmer, better pages with a bit of effort, and a framework for building the fully featured pages an end user will demand.

The implementation uses TclOO for a base class with mixins to provide customized behavior for particular database engines. The test engines are sqlite3 and TDBC.

1 Introduction

One application of the 80/20 rule is that 80 percent of an application is the code that's boring to write, and 20 percent will be fun. In a database application with many data entry screens this ratio could push 95-5.

It would be nice if the 95 percent part of a database application could be generated without requiring 95 percent of the programmer's time.

It turns out that this can be done.

There is enough information in an SQL schema to create a simple entry screen. The following schema can be used to generate an adequate GUI:

```
table create phoneList {
  id integer unique,
  name text,  -- person
  phone text, -- phone number
  type text -- home, work, mobile
}
```

The GUI would resemble:

Figure 1: Simple, uninstrumented GUI

By adding some extra information about the fields, the GUI can be improved to resemble the following image:

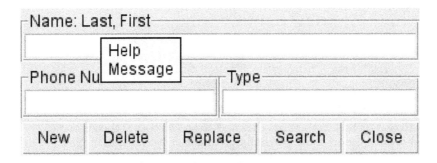

Figure 2: Simple, instrumented GUI

To paraphrase many lolcats, *Simple tables are Simple*. In order to be useful, the EditTables package needed handle one-to-one mapping schemas, such those containing references to other tables.

```
table create phoneList {
  id integer unique,
  name text,
  num  text,
  typeid integer references types
}
```

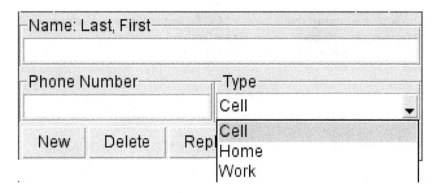

Figure 3: Reference, instrumented GUI

The package also needs to handle many-to-one mapping, perhaps a fixed number of fields as shown below:

```
table create person {
     id integer unique,
     name text,
     address text,
   }
 }
table create phone {
     id integer unique,
     num  text,
     personid integer references person,
     typeid integer references types
   }
```

Figure 4: Reference to table, instrumented GUI

The trick to generating these sorts of GUI's instead of just a simple GUI from the pure schema requires adding some layout instructions.

The next requirement is to validate inputs. This may need to be done on a per-field basis, or when the user submits a page. Both of these options are supported in this package.

Finally, a useful package needs to work with multiple database back ends. It would be nice to only support TDBC, but in the real world, TDBC doesn't have enough penetration (yet).

There are features in Tcl 8.6 that allow all of the requirements to be met.

The package is written using TclOO. The base package understands Tk and how an SQL schema is laid out. It provides some primitives that the other classes can use to find a primary field, find references, etc.

If the project starts using the `EditTable` package, the layout instructions can be embedded into the SQL schema and extracted as needed. If `EditTable` is being shoe-horned onto an existing database, or if you find the idea of mixing layout commands and data definitions distasteful, the instrumentation can be provided by modifying the method that acquires the layout commands in the Tcl object.

Validation is accomplished by adding flags to fields with some common validation routines available in the main class, and the capability of adding custom validation if an application requires it.

Finally, support for multiple database backends is accomplished using TclOO's `mixin` feature.

The current version of `editTable` is the fourth or fifth iteration of ideas. It's being used in a commercial product. It's also likely to see a number of modifications before it gets used in another product.

2 Using `EditTable` **package**

2.1 Creation

The `EditTable` package is constructed using the TclOO megawidget design pattern described by Donal Fellows (Tcl/Tk Proceedings 2009) and in my book (`Tcl/Tk: A Developer's Guide`, Chapter 11). This pattern emulates a standard Tcl widget, allowing the new `editTable` object to be created like any other Tk widget.

Syntax: editTable *widgetName mixin dbEngine args*

widgetName	Name of the widget, normal Tk style
mixin	Name of the db engine mixin
dbEngine	Name of the db engine to use
args	Optional arguments for opening the db engine

Creating an `editTable` connected to an SQLite database named `test.db` would resemble:

```
set obj [editTable .t1 SQLITE3_support sqlite3 -dbArgs test.db]
```

Doing the same with a TDBC engine that's connected to the SQLite database would resemble:

```
set obj [editTable .t1 TDBC_support sqlite3 test.db]
```

Once an `editTable` object has been created, it can be used to query various parameters using the `config` or `configure` commands (both map to the same underlying code.)

Like Tk, the `configure` command will accept no arguments to return all configuration options and values, a single argument to report the value of an option, or a pair of arguments to set a value.

One of the options that can be extracted is the underlying database pointer. Extracting this allows an application to interact directely with the database object opened by `editTable`. This end-run functionality allows applications to easily extend the behavior of the `editTable` class.

The next snippet shows creating an `editTable` object, extracting the TDBC database object and using that to create a table in the underlying sqlite3 database.

```
set obj [editTable .t1 TDBC_support sqlite3 test.db]
set db [$obj config db]
$db allrows {
  CREATE TABLE person (
    id integer unique primary key,
    loginid text, -- loginID
    fname text, -- First name
    lname text, -- Last name
    addrRef integer references addr
    );
}
```

There are several methods defined for the `editTable` object. The most commonly used are:

- *editObj* config

- *editObj* getSchema

- *editObj* makeGUI

- *editObj* populateBySearch

The config command will let the application query or set configuration options. If it is called with no key, it will return a list of all currently defined keys and values.

Syntax: `editObj` *config ?key? ?value?*

editObj	A widget created with `editTable` command
config	Query or set a config option
key	Name of the config option or blank
?value?	Optional value to define an option

The `getSchema` method will retrieve a schema for a table from the database, or optional schema retrieval process. The default behavior is to query the database. This is used internally to build GUIs for tables containing relations.

Syntax: `editObj` *getSchema tableName*

editObj	A widget created with `editTable` command
getSchema	Return the schema for a table
tableName	Name of the table to return Schema for

The `makeGUI` method is the workhorse that builds a GUI within the `editTable` frame. It can build a GUI for any table defined within the database. The `editTable` object can rebuild itself to display a different table as necessary. The default GUI includes buttons to perform simple searches, and add, delete or modify a record.

Syntax: `editObj` *makeGUI schema*

editObj	A widget created with `editTable` command
makeGUI	Construct a GUI within the editTable object frame.
schema	a Schema - may be return from `getSchema`

The `populateBySearch` method will load values into the fields of a GUI. The query can be any valid query suitable for an SQL `SELECT` on the currently active table.

Syntax: `editObj` *populateBySearch query*

editObj	A widget created with `editTable` command
populateBySearch	Populates the values in a GUI
query	An SQL query

The next example shows initializing a sample database and creating a simple GUI for a table.

```
toplevel .tt
set obj [editTable .tt.t1 TDBC_support sqlite3 -dbArgs test2.db]
set db [$obj config db]

$db allrows {
  CREATE TABLE person (
    id integer unique primary key,
```

```
        loginid text, -- loginID
        fname text, -- First name
        lname text, -- Last name
        addrRef integer references addr
        );
        CREATE TABLE addr (
        id integer unique primary key,
        street text, -- Address
        city text, -- Address
        state text -- Address
    )
}

$db allrows {INSERT INTO addr VALUES (1, '123 St', 'Acity', 'AA')}
$db allrows {INSERT INTO addr VALUES (2, '234 St', 'Bcity', 'BB')}
$db allrows {INSERT INTO person VALUES (1, 'aaa', 'Alpha', 'Adam', 1)}
$db allrows {INSERT INTO person VALUES (2, 'bbb', 'Beta', 'Blocker', 2)}
$db allrows {INSERT INTO person VALUES (3, 'aa2', 'Abel', 'Adam', 2)}
$db allrows {INSERT INTO person VALUES (4, 'aa3', 'Aard', 'Adam', 2)}

$obj makeGUI [$obj getSchema person]
$obj config -table person
$obj populateBySearch "loginid = 'aaa'"

pack .tt.t1
```

The generated GUI resembles this:

Figure 5: default GUI

2.2 Layout Information

Because we are polite and civilized, we will not call the previous example butt-ugly.

But it is.

An SQL schema is designed to convey the logical date relationships between fields and tables. It is not designed to convey any information about aesthetics.

The aesthetic information is conveyed as a six element list attached to each field that is to be displayed. The elements are shown in the following list. The first 2 are required, the others have default values that may be adequate.

help	A message to display in a popup help balloon
label	The label to display with this field
reference	If this field references another table, this element will contain the `table.field` name of the referenced table. If this field contains non-referential data, this element is blank.
widget arguments	arguments for the entry or combobox widget that will be created. These might include `-width` or `-background` arguments.
row column	A list of the row and column where this field is to be displayed.
grid options	Arguments to be attached to a grid command for this field. These might include `-columnspan` for example.

This technique for conveying layout info is sub-optimal. The requirements grew as the complexity of the application grew.

But it works.

The layout information is included in a Schema by adopting a modification of the standard SQL comment.

An instrumented schema has the layout string appended to a field definition with a triple-dash comment.

A simple GUI can be created like this:

```
set obj [editTable .t1 "" "" -table phoneList]

$obj makeGUI {
 table create phoneList (
 id integer unique,
 name text,  --- {First Last} {Name} {} {-width 40} {1 1} {-columnspan 2}
 num  text, --- {Number with area code} {Phone Number} {} {} {2 1}
 type text  --- {Type of phone} {Type} {} {} {2 2}
 );
}

grid .t1
```

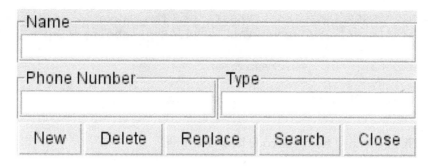

Figure 6: simple GUI with layout info

The editTable widget requires that the SQL schema follow strict rules and a field which references another table must include a *references* clause.

The presence or absense of the *references* clause determines how the third field - the reference element is to be treated.

If a *references* clause is present, then the reference element contains the database field name, or list of field names, to display in each element of a combobox. The fields to display must be named as tableName.fieldName.

One pattern used with references is for a table to reference one of several options. The next example is a database in which the book table has a string for title and a reference for author. The author table has separate fields for first and last name. The combination of first and last is displayed in the combobox for selecting an author.

```
set obj [editTable .book SQLITE3_support sqlite3 -dbArgs test4.db]
set db [$obj config db]

$db eval {
CREATE TABLE book (
id integer unique primary key,
title text, --- {} {Title} {} {-width 40} {1 1} {-columnspan 2}
authorid integer references author
    --- {} {Author} {author.first author.last} {} {2 1}
);

CREATE TABLE author (
id integer unique primary key,
first text, --- {First Name} {First} {}
last text  --- {Last Name} {Last} {}
);
}

$db eval "INSERT INTO author VALUES (1, 'Clif', 'Flynt')"
$db eval "INSERT INTO author VALUES (2, 'Mark', 'Twain')"
$db eval "INSERT INTO book VALUES (1,'Tcl/Tk: A Developer''s Guide', 1)"
```

```
$db eval "INSERT INTO book VALUES (2,'Tom Sawyer', 2)"
$db eval "INSERT INTO book VALUES (3,'Huckleberry Finn', 2)"

$obj makeGUI [$obj getSchema book]
$obj config -table book
$obj populateBySearch "title like '%Tcl%'"
grid .book
```

The GUI generated from this code looks like this:

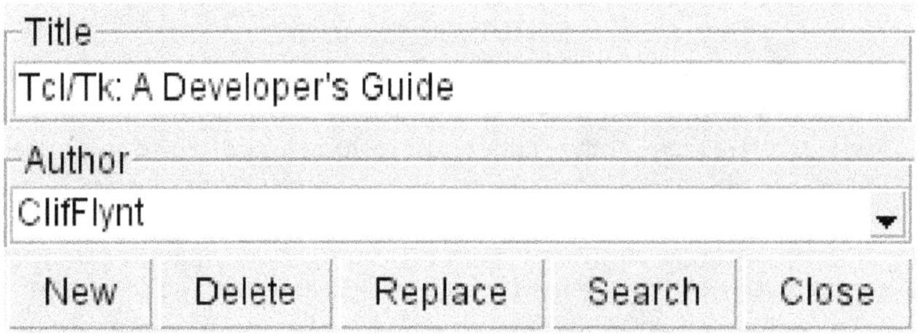

Figure 7: Schema with reference and layout info

Another common pattern is the many-to-one mapping implemented by having a field in one table point back to another table. In a book database, there are an undefined number of keywords that might be attached to a book.

The schema for this pattern would resemble:

```
CREATE TABLE book (
  id integer unique primary key,
  title text,
);
CREATE TABLE keyword (
  id integer unique primary key,
  key text,
  bookid integer references book
);
```

To generate a GUI for this database pattern, the reference element in the layout field in the keyword table is used to hold the name of a table. When a GUI is generated for a table listed in the reference element, an *Associated values* section is created in the GUI.

Expanding the previous example to include a reference table, the new table resembles this

```
CREATE TABLE keyword (
  id integer unique primary key,
```

```
   key text,  --- {Keyword} {Category} {book} {} {}
   bookid integer references book --- {book} {Title} {book.title} {} {}
);
```

Which creates the following GUI:

Figure 8: Schema with reference and layout info

The E button in the previous image opens a new toplevel to edit a keyword which will be associated with this table row.

2.3 Customization

The `editTable` widget follows the Tk dictum of being adequate with no tweaking, and open for customization if the application isn't suited to the base GUI.

Various degrees of customization are supported. These techniques include:

- using the layout elements

- configuring options for screen or field validation

- building a separate mix-in or inherited class

- tweaking the GUI before using it

Using layout elements to modify the appearance of the GUI works as described.

By default, a `editTable` GUI has no validation. Per-Field validation can be enabled by configuring the `validate, fieldName` attributes for a GUI. The validation attributes accept a script to evaluate when focus leaves that field. The widget name (entry or combobox) and field name are appended to the script when it's invoked.

The `editTable` class includes some trivial validation methods including `validatePhone` and `validateNumeric`.

2.4 Extending the class

The current implementation of `editTable` has mixins for Sqlite3 and TDBC. A programmer can add a new mixin to support another database engine by coding the engine-specific methods:

`init`	Initialize a connection to the database.
`getSchema`	Retrieve the schema for a given table. Setting `save` sets this to be the active table.)
`doSQL`	Execute an SQL command and return whatever the command returns. This provides a generic access to the underlying database.
`getTables`	Return a list of the tables defined by this database.
`getPrimary`	Retrieve the name of the primary key.
`doReplace`	Update the DB row based on the contents of the GUI.
`doNew`	Create a new row in the DB based on the contents of the GUI.
`populateBySearch`	Populate the GUI based on an SQL query.
`getValues`	Return a set of values based on a list of `tableName.fieldName` values
`getValueByRef`	Returns a value from table `$tbl` for field `$fld` where the primary is `$value`
`populateWithFwdRef`	Populate a GUI that includes forward references based on an SQL query
`closeDB`	Close the connection to the DB

2.4.1 GUI Modification

Since the GUI follows a fixed pattern, it can be modified post-`makeGUI` and before display.

For example, if users are only allowed to view and edit fields, the the delete button can be removed with a command like:

```
$obj makeGUI $specialSchema noClose
$obj configure -table book
```

Getting more aggressive, rather than showing the *Associated values* for a row, as they are displayed by default, an application can define a fixed quantity of associated values and a custom display procedure while taking advantage of the bulk of the `editTables` widget.

The next example demonstrates a book database that emulates a card catalog via a slider on the side to select books, and a simplified display of keywords.

It does this by with a special procedure to construct the GUI and a new procedure to extend the normal editTable population methods. The new procedure for creating the GUI (bldBookGUI) defines a modified schema with a couple extra fields to hold the keywords. The showItem procedure uses the populateBySearch method to populate the fields that are defined in the book schema, and has extra code to populate the extra fields.

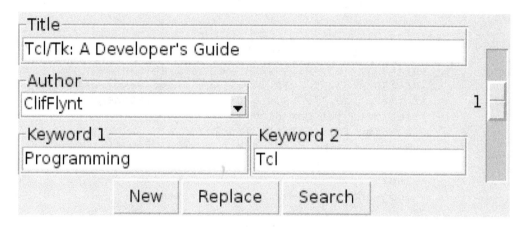

Figure 9: Schema with reference and layout info

```
toplevel .t3

set obj [editTable .t3.t2 SQLITE3_support sqlite3 -dbArgs test3.db]

proc bldBookGUI {obj} {
  set specialSchema {
 CREATE TABLE book (
   id integer unique primary key,
   title text, --- {Title} {Title} {} {-width 40} {1 1} {-columnspan 2}
   authorid integer references author, --- {Author} {Author} {author.first autho
   keyword1 text --- {Keyword} {Keyword 1} {keyword.key} {} {3 1}
   keyword2 text --- {Keyword} {Keyword 2} {keyword.key} {} {3 2}
 );
  }

  $obj makeGUI $specialSchema noClose
  $obj configure -table book
  destroy $obj.buttons.b_Delete
```

```
    set prim [$obj getPrimary book]
    set count [$obj doSQL "SELECT count($prim) FROM book"]

    set scale [scale .t3.sc -from 0 -to $count \
        -command [list showItem $obj $specialSchema .t3.sc ]]
    grid $obj $scale
}

proc showItem {obj schema scale num} {
    $obj populateBySearch "id=$num"

    set pos 0
    foreach l [split $schema \n] {
        lassign [$obj splitSchemaLine $l] def layout
        lassign $layout help label ref args rowcol grid0
        if {($ref ne "") && ([string first "references" $l] < 0)} {
            set dfld [lindex $l 0]
            lassign [split $ref .] tbl fld
            set lst [$obj doSQL "SELECT $fld FROM $tbl WHERE bookid=$num"]
            set item [lindex $lst $pos]
            incr pos
            $obj configure -value,$dfld $item

        }

    }
}
bldBookGUI $obj
```

3 Implementation

The editTable widget is implemented as a TclOO Megawidget with mixins to provide database engine customization.

Another standard pattern would have been to make each database engine a class that inherited the base functions from editTable. I considered and discarded this pattern in order to have a single widget class (editTable) rather than multiple classes (editSQLite, editTDBC, etc.).

The editTable class uses the technique for creating a megawidget described by Donal Fellows in his 2009 paper, and also described in my book (Tcl/Tk: A Developer's Guide, Chapter 11) (Shameless plug).

This technique uses a classmethod call to create an unknown method that checks to see if the first argument is a window name, and if so proceeds to create the new widget.

```
# Create a class method
# Avoid redefining classmethod if it already exists.
if {[info proc ::oo::define::classmethod] eq ""} {
proc ::oo::define::classmethod {name {args ""} {body ""}} {
    # Create the method on the class if the caller gave
    # arguments and body
    if {[llength [info level 0]] == 4} {
        uplevel 1 [list self method $name $args $body]
    }
    # Get the name of the class being defined
    set cls [lindex [info level -1] 1]
    # Make connection to private class "my" command by
    # forwarding
    uplevel forward $name [info object namespace $cls]::my $name
}
}


oo::class create editTable {
  classmethod unknown {w args} {
# puts "UNKL: $w -- $args"
    if {[string match .* $w]} {
      [self] new $w {*}$args
      return $w
    }
    next $w {*}$args
  }
...
}
```

When a new instance is created, one of the arguments describes the mixin to be added. Since mixins don't have constructors, the editTable constructor calls a init method defined within the mixin to perform special initializations.

The editTable class can create objects that have lives of their own. These includes GUI widgets, open database connections and may include slaved editTable GUIs. Because of these additional elements to the editTable class, the editTable class requires a destructor.

Each editTable object contains a list of cloned and referenced objects. The desstructor descends upon these like a wolf upon the fold destroying them in gay abandon.

While the editTable class is happy to have multiple channels to databases, many database engines are less happy with this. The init method in the mixins avoids opening multiple channels. The editTable class must also avoid closing a database channel until all users have been destroyed.

A class variable is used to keep track of the number of open database connections. Again, this code was stolen from Donal Fellows' 2009 talk and my book.

```
if {[info proc ::oo::Helpers::classvar] eq ""} {
proc ::oo::Helpers::classvar {args} {
    # Get reference to classs namespace
    set ns [info object namespace [uplevel 1 {self class}]]
    # Double up the list of varnames
    foreach v $args {
      uplevel 1 namespace upvar $ns $v $v
    }
}
}
```

4   Future

The method of conveying the layout information, and what information is required has been evolutionary. It is subject to a rework before the this package gets used in another application.

The schema parsing is a quick and dirty approach that assumes each field definition is contained on a single line. The schema parsing will be enhanced as a method of the base editTable class.

It may be possible to reduce the number of methods in the mixin classes by better use of the basic methods in the editTables class.

5   Summary

The current status of the editTable class is *functional*. It's in use in a commercial product and is scheduled for a several other in-house and out-house projects.

What started as a simple way to generate a *good enough* GUI that reflected the underlying database schema has expanded into a package that can generate a commercial-grade GUI with capability of hiding the schema and providing a simple interface to a user.

The underlying simple display has been retained with potential tweaks to extend the behavior beyond simple.

As the class is force-fed to other applications I expect to discover more things it *should* do, and streamline the current feature set.

The current escape is available at http://www.noucorp.com.

Customizable Keyboard Shortcuts

Ron Wold
Mentor Graphics Corporation
8005 SW Boeckman Road
Wilsonville, OR 97070
503-685-0878

Abstract

Anyone that spends a lot of time using the same software tool becomes very familiar with it. They know how the tool works, what the tool's commands are and when to execute these commands. Coined a "power user", these type of users operates fast. Power users want quick access to commands, they do not want to navigate through a menu to access commonly used operations. User interfaces often address this issue by adding toolbar buttons, but, the fastest method of access is through a keyboard shortcut.

A keyboard shortcut refers to the association of a key sequence with an operation. User interfaces typically have a predefined set of keyboard shortcuts. However, a tool that runs on multiple platforms and that has dozens of windows and hundreds of operations will be unable to define a single set of shortcuts that is sufficient for all users.

Modelsim is a software program written in Tcl/Tk that has been recently enhanced to support customizable keyboard shortcuts. Users can associate a key sequence with a menu pick, a toolbar button, a CLI command or a custom tcl script. In addition, users can specify that the key sequence is applicable for the entire tool or for just a specific window. Implementing this functionality presented several technical challenges. Tcl/Tk has a unique methodology for processing keyboard events and a successful solution requires an architecture that functions within the bounds of this methodology. This paper will discuss the basic architecture as well as the technical challenges that were faced and how they were addressed.

Keywords

Tcl/Tk, keyboard shortcuts, bind, bindtags, customizable

1. Introduction

Modelsim is an integrated development environment (IDE) used by electronic designers to develop, debug, simulate and test electronic designs. It supports several different hardware description languages (HDLs) - such as VHDL [1] and Verilog [2]. Modelsim's user interface is comprised of many unique windows, toolbars, menus, popups and a command line interface. The user interface is written entirely in Tcl/Tk.

Developing a functional, well tested electronic design can take several weeks to several months. Users that spend this much time working with the same tool become 'power users' [3]. A key behavior of a power user is their desire to perform operations quickly. Within a graphical user interface, there are many ways to perform an operation such as selecting a menu item from a popup, clicking a tool bar or by typing the command into a command line interface. While each of these methods has their advantages, none of methods can be executed as quickly as a keyboard shortcut.

A keyboard shortcut[4] is a key combination that performs a certain command. The efficiency of a shortcut key comes from that fact that it can be invoked entirely from the keyboard. A user isn't required to position the mouse cursor or click mouse buttons.

Keyboard shortcuts are not a new concept. On some platforms, such as Microsoft Windows ™, there is a standard set of keyboard shortcuts. Given an operating system, a tool developer can identify the common shortcuts and implement them within their tool. However, a conflict can arise if the tool supports multiple platforms, and the standard shortcuts are different between the two platforms. For many years Modelsim detected the platform that was in use and defined the shortcuts based on the platform. Although this is more flexible than a single shortcut definition, the solution is still incomplete. Users want a shortcut definition that matches their own expectations, and they want shortcuts for the commands that they most often use. Since there is not a single set of keyboard shortcuts that will appease all 'power users', the best solution is to allow users to define and customize their own shortcuts.

2. Shortcut Fundamentals

Implementing a shortcut in Tcl/Tk requires the bind[5] command. In its simplest form, the bind command associates an event, like a key stroke or mouse event, with an action, like a procedure call. For example, consider this bind command:

```
bind .a.b.c <control-key-x> "Control_X_pressed"
```

This bind will result in the procedure "Control_X_pressed" being called when the widget .a.b.c receives the control-x key. In this example, the binding is placed on the widget .a.b.c, but bindings can also be placed on the name of a widget class. When a binding is placed on the name of a widget class, all instances of that widget inherit the binding. A binding can also be placed on "all" which causes all widgets to inherit the binding. Widgets also have the notion of bindtags. A widget's bind tags is a list of tag names, which may include the widget's name, that class name and all.

```
bindtags .a.b.c {.a.b.c My_Class . all }
```

When an event occurs on a widget, it is applied to each of the window's bind tags, in the order in which they are defined. If the bind tag has a binding definition for the event, then the bindtag's script is executed.

3. Capturing keyboard events

Modelsim's user interface is comprised of many windows. These windows are actually just widgets that contain other widgets, but from a user's standpoint, a window is a self contained tool providing specific functionality.

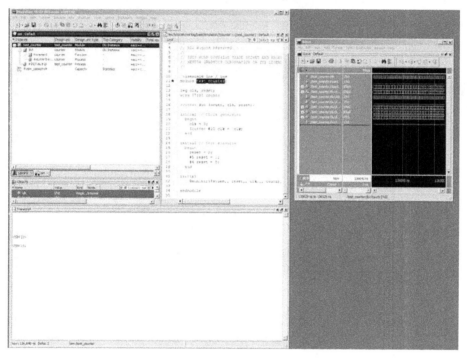

Figure 1 - Modelsim Windows

When a user activates a particular window and issues a keyboard event, such as key-delete, there is an expectation that whatever is selected in the window will be deleted. However, a window may be comprised of multiple subwidgets and each subwidget can take focus and thus be the target of the keyboard event. The user may have activated the window by clicking in any of the subwidgets. From the users standpoint, the shortcut key is defined by the window, not the individual subwidgets that make up the window. This creates a technical challenge in that every subwidget must have an identical binding. There are other possible solutions, such as forcing focus to a particular widget which contains the correct bindings, but these solutions require a detailed understanding of a window's construction. Modelsim has over 50 distinct windows, so defining a customizable binding architecture that requires significant window specific changes is not feasible given this project's time constraints.

Rather than managing the customizable bindings on a widget, an alternative approach was taken. Applying a binding to the 'all' tag provides a means of catching an event that is independent of the target widget. Given the following bind command:

```
bind all <key-delete> "Binding::ServiceBinding %W $key %k %x %y %X %Y %A"
```

a user can click anywhere in a window that is comprised of subwidgets, hit the delete key, and the procedure Binding::ServiceBinding will be executed. There are, however, two exceptions. The first is that all widgets must have the 'all' tag in their list of bindtags. This is not an issue with the Modelsim environment. Widgets receive the 'all' bind tag by default, and this bind tag is not removed from any widget. The second issue that can prevent the 'all' tag from receiving an event occurs if there is a binding for an event on one of the bind tags found earlier in the bind tag list and the binding script issues a break. For example, given these definitions:

```
bind .a.b.c <key-delete> "Delete_Something;break"
bind all <key-delete> "Binding::ServiceBinding %W <key-delete>"
bindtags .a.b.c { .a.b.c all}
```

the call to Binding::ServiceBinding will never occur. The binding tag .a.b.c is found earlier in the bind tag list than the bind tag all, so it is executed first. Since the binding script contains a break, all bindtag processes are halted. This behavior is fundamental to Tcl/Tk's bind processing algorthim, and the only way to assure that Binding::ServiceBinding is executed is by eliminating the break. The example below replaces the bind command on the widget with a procedure call, Binding::DefineBinding:

```
Binding::DefineBinding .a.b.c <key-delete> "Delete_Something"
bind all <key-delete> "Binding::ServiceBinding %W <key-delete>"
bindtags .a.b.c { .a.b.c all}
```

Replacing the bind call with a call to Binding::DefineBinding serves two purposes. First it eliminates the binding conflict between the .a.b.c tag and the all tag. More importantly, it captures and stores the *intent* of the original bind command. In this example, the intent can be described as *"if widget .a.b.c is the target widget and the delete key is hit, the procedure Delete_Something should be called"*. When Binding::ServiceBinding recieves an event, it compares the target widget and the key event with the binding defintions that have been defined via Binding::DefineBinding command. If a match is found, the script associated with the binding definition is executed.

4. The Binding database

Replacing a bind command with a command that saves the bind's intentions results in a database of binding definitions. Not all bind commands use the bind database. Many bind commands are not candidates for shortcut keys, such as binds that are based on mouse buttons or motion events. For example, the right mouse button raises a window's popup. If a user changed this binding they could lose access to the popup menu. Only bindings that are intended as a shortcut key are stored in the binding database.

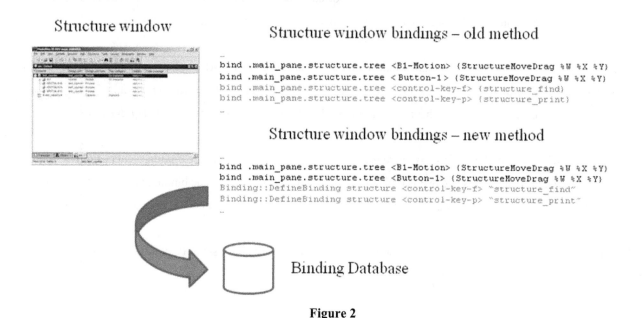

Figure 2

Storing binding definitions in a database has several advantages. First, changing a binding involves nothing more than changing the database. Since the bindings are no longer placed directly on widgets, knowledge of a window's widget hierarchy is not required when modify or adding a binding definition. The database also allows for persistent storage and binding definitions can easily be imported and exported. Lastly, determining what shortcuts are available in any given window becomes a trivial task.

5. Processing a keyboard event

The following tcl code creates a binding on the bindtag `all`. The binding will be in place for all widgets that currently exist as well as any widget created in the future.

```
foreach key [Supported_Shorcut_Keys] {
    bind all $key "Binding::ServiceBinding %W $key %k %x %y %X %Y %A"
}
```

When a shortcut key event occurs, regardless of the target widget, `Binding::ServiceBinding will` catch the event. `Binding::ServiceBinding` then examines the binding database and determines if there is a binding script associated with the event. If there is an associated script, the script is invoked.

6. Binding Priority

Modelsim is comprised of many windows. Each window has commands that are specific to only that window as well as keyboard shortcuts that reference these commands. Executing a window specific command requires that the window be activated. Likewise, a window's keyboard shortcut is only valid if the window that it is associated with it is active. Binding definitions that are associated with a particular window are called *window bindings*.

There are, however, commands that are not window specific. These commands are available without regard to the active window. For example, Modelsim's 'open' command will open a source file for editing and this command is always available. Binding definitions that are not associated with a specific window are called *global bindings*.

In addition to window and global bindings, there is also a distinction between intrinsic bindings and custom bindings. An *intrinsic* binding is one that is defined by a tool developer. An intrinsic binding is built into the tool and it is available to a user the first time they run Modelsim. A binding that a user adds is called a *custom* binding.

The distinction between window and global bindings and whether they are intrinsic or custom is important when an event matches more than one binding definition.

Consider the following scenario; a global intrinsic binding is added by a developer, say control-s, which raises a generic search dialog. In addition, a window intrinsic binding is added by a developer to the source window, it also uses control-s, but the bind script is different, it issues a command to save outstanding edits. Next, a user redefines the control-s binding definition for the source window to yet another command. When the user opens a source file and issues control-s, `Binding::ServiceBinding` will be called and it will examine the binding definitions database, looking for a match. This search will result in three matches, each with a different binding script. Only one of the binding scripts should execute, determining which binding definition to execute requires rules of priority. There are four categories of binding definitions, intrinsic global, custom global, intrinsic window and custom window. Given these four categories, we concluded that a window binding definition has precedence over a global binding definition and that a custom binding definition has precedence over an intrinsic binding definition. Implementing these rules of priority results in the following order of precedence. (Figure 3).

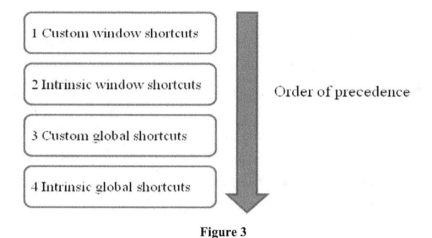

Figure 3

7. Editing the binding definition database

With an architecture that supports customized keyboard shortcuts, the final requirement is defining a user interface for adding, modifying and deleting keyboard shortcuts. The user interface must present the information found in the binding database in an understandable form, as well as provide operations for adding and modifying the database.

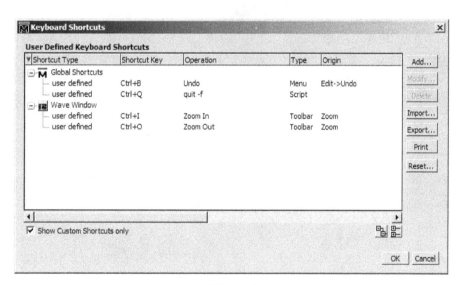

Figure 4

The keyboard shortcut dialog (Figure 4) lists the shortcuts found in the binding database. By default, only shortcuts added by the user are listed. Unchecking the check box 'Show Custom Shortcuts only' will cause intrinsic shortcuts to be displayed as well. Shortcuts are grouped by the window that they are associated with or as a global shortcut. A keyboard shortcut list item displays its shortcut type, the associated shortcut key, as well as information on the menu item or toolbar that the key is associated with.

Adding a keyboard shortcut is nothing more than adding a new entry in the binding database. From a user's standpoint, they simply want to associate a key sequence with a menu item, toolbar button or a tcl script. This simplistic requirement contains a technical challenge; specifically how does one present a user with a complete list of menu items and toolbar buttons?

A fewl years ago Modelsim's user interface underwent a re-architecture to address issues due to an ever increasing number of windows[7]. This re-architecture included a well defined API for creating menus, menu items and toolbars. The API is essentially a group of wrapper functions that embed the actual Tk menu functions. Since these wrapper functions are used for all menu and toolbar creation, they provide a single point for capturing and saving menu creation and hierarchy.

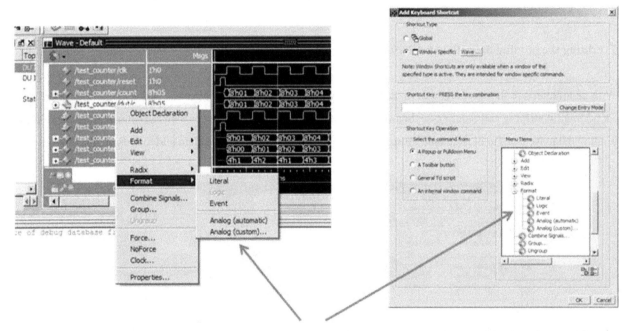

The menu items and their commands are captured at the time of creation. This data is used later by the "Add Keyboard Shortcut" dialog, providing a list of menu items that can be selected.

It is important to display menu items using the same name and hierarchy that is found in the menu itself. This is also true for toolbars, their name and listing order must also match the actual toolbar. Matching hierarchy makes finding the menu item or toolbar much easier.

8. Teaching the shortcuts

If a user is not aware of a keyboard shortcut, the shortcut will not be used. Although a listing of intrinsic shortcuts can be found in Modelsim's documentation, quite often users do not read the documentation. Modelsim has two features that are intended to help users learn the available shortcuts.

Keyboard Shortcut Quick Help

Modelsim has an intrinsic keyboard shortcut that will raise a temporary dialog. This dialog lists the keyboard shortcuts that are currently available for the active window.

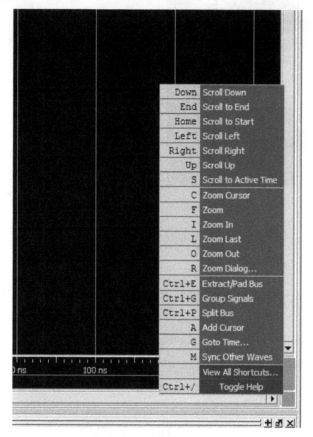

Figure 5 Keyboard Shortcut Quick Help

Dynamic Menu Item shortcut key association

If a menu item has an associated shortcut key, it has become common practice to display the key sequence to the right of the menu item text. We modified our default menu post command to query the default binding database before rendering each menu item. If a menu item has an associated shortcut key, the shortcut key is displayed to the right the menu text. The shortcut key display is dynamic in that it is not statically defined with the menu item. If a user changes or deletes a shortcut key, the associated menu item will reflect the change immediately.

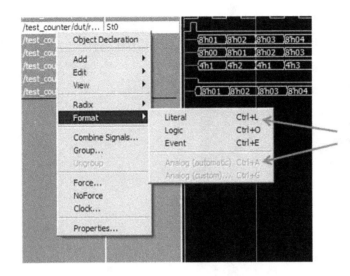

Menu items display the shortcut key that is associated with the item

9. Issues

Custom Window Bindings

When a user creates a custom window binding, they must specify the window type. If they are adding a custom binding to a menu or toolbar, the dialog provides a list of menu items or toolbars to select from. The list of menu items or toolbars is created when the menu item or toolbars is created. If a menu hasn't been created it will not be in the list that the user can select from. If a window has not been opened at least once, there will be no information to display in the add shortcut key dialog. We address this issue when the user selects the window type that they want to apply the binding to. The user selects from a list of window types and only windows that have been instanced at least once in the current session can be chosen. This solution is not ideal, but Modelsim's user interface must support 3rd party windows seamlessly and this approach achieves this.

Dialogs and in place edit boxes

Adding a binding to the "all" bindtag generates a lot of event traffic sent to `Binding::ServiceBinding`. The traffic does not generate a performance issue, but there are situations where the active window and the shortcut key match a binding definition, but the binding script should not be executed. A text entry box in a dialog is one example. Modelsim follows a model dialog model. When a dialog is raised, all key events are intended for the dialog, not the underlying window. The service binding routine must first detect whether a dialog is raised before processing a key event. When a dialog is raised and a key is detected, all key events received by the service routine are ignored..

An even more difficult issue occurs when in-place text entry boxes are used. Several of Modelsim's windows use in-place text boxes. For example, when the user double clicks on some text, a text box is placed directly on the window. Unlike a dialog, detecting a text entry box requires examining the widget class name. The service routine must exclude processing for certain class names.

Context specific menus

Context menus are created on the fly, the menu items are typically based upon a current state within the window, such as selection. Context specific menu items are cleared and recreated each time the menu is raised. For example, consider a debugger's breakpoint menu, when the user places the mouse over a visual break point and issues the popup, the menu items are created based upon the specific breakpoint. The menu items could have the name of the breakpoint in the menu text, as well as in the menu command. This type of menu item is not a candidate for a keyboard shortcut and special work is needed to prevent a user from binding to the menu item.

10.0 References

[1] Doulos, A Brief History of VHDL, http://www.doulos.com/fi/desguidevhdl/vb2_history.htm.

[2] Doulos, A Brief History of Verilog, http://www.doulos.com/fi/desguidevlg/vb2_history.htm

[3] http://en.wikipedia.org/wiki/Power_user

[4] http://www.techterms.com/definition/keyboardshortcut

[5] http://www.tcl.tk/man/tcl8.5/TkCmd/bind.htm

[6] http://www.tcl.tk/man/tcl8.5/TkCmd/bindtags.htm

[7] Too Many Windows, Ron Wold, 2010 Tcl/Tk Conference.

Tcl 2012
Chicago, IL
November 14-16, 2012

Session 7
November 16 10:45-12:15

A Guided debugging of EDA software with various components of Tcl/Tk GUI

Roshni Lalwani

roshni_lalwani@mentor.com

Amarpal Singh

amarpal_singh@mentor.com

Abstract

EDA software has various hardware design rule checks that can be debugged easily using schematic widget. The main objective of design rule checking (DRC) is to achieve a high overall yield and reliability for a hardware design. If design rules are violated the design may not be functional at all. This paper presents a flow of using some enhanced Tcl/Tk widgets in an innovate manner that can facilitate hardware designers in debugging various design issues of EDA tools.

1. Introduction

Our Tcl/Tk based GUI software provides a debugging environment to various EDA tools. It is built upon various widgets like schematic widget, dialog boxes, MTIwidgets etc. A schematic generator widget (Nlview) is a visualization software component that helps electronic design engineers to easily understand, debug, optimize and document electronic designs. A schematic window in a Tcl/Tk GUI is a simplified graphical representation of an electrical circuit .The schematic diagram consists of instances, pins and nets that are graphical representation of hardware design netlist. The schematic widget supports a number of features to navigate the user to **interesting parts** of the logic and to present engineering information in relation to the schematic. The Schematic Generator is not intended to extract any engineering data from the netlist - but is designed to generate a schematic as a **"skeleton"** for presenting these data. This implies the need of an engineering system that "feeds" Nlview with data. The data is provided by various EDA tools via our GUI interface. The interface between Schematic Generator and Our Tcl/Tk based GUI is defined by string based API (Application Programming Interface). These APIs provides a simple set of commands, callbacks and configuration properties and makes it easy to visualize and debug the EDA software backend data.

There are certain attributes associated with each HDL components/objects like instances, pins and nets. The idea here is to display this information in the callout box on various objects of the schematic window, in such a way that it will help the user in debugging the problematic design issues. A callout box in schematic window is sticky tag visually associated with each object in the schematic window. A callout box is a nothing but a pixmap formed by few rendering shape and text rendering APIs, so it is very fast and efficient. The call out box is a light weight object that can be displayed on any object in the schematic. It displays the text that gives a user a way to solve the DRCs and other design issues. The callout box is integrated in our Tcl/Tk GUI using Tcl/Tk interface provided by NLview widget.

Section 2 below covers callout box, highlighting how callout box helps in debugging design rules checks and **Section 3** outlines the enhanced dialogue box and its integration with the callout box functionality.

2. <u>Guided debugging using Callout Box</u>

A design rule error is often associated with one or two instances. There is an error instance where rule error occurs and there is source instance that is starting pointing for the error. For example, there is design rule error which reports a wrong simulation value at the input pin of error instance. The incorrect simulation value is because the source instance and error instance are clocked by same clock. The tool also displays callout box on source and error instance. The message displayed in callout box is an intuitive step to debug and resolve the design rule error. There are also attributes associated with source and error instances. This information is also displayed on the source and error instances in the same callout box.

For example the schematic view with callout box is as follows.

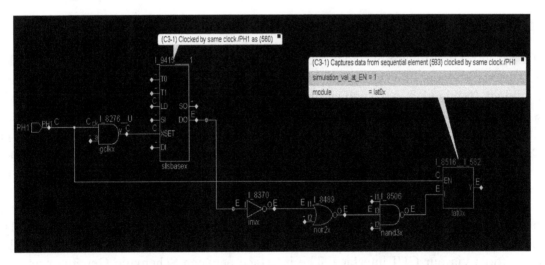

2.1. **Callout box Integration in with GUI tool**

The schematic generator component integrated with our GUI tool provides an API based mechanism to attach various kinds of attributes with Schematic objects like instances, pins nets. These attributes can be visual or only non-visual in nature. The various kind of visual attributes are like object's display name, object's border color, object's fill color and object's line style (solid/dashed/thick/thin etc). Outbox is also one special kind of visual attribute attached to Nlview objects where application can along with specifying the text to be shown in an outbox, configure the outbox for its background color, foreground color and color of its various regions. Mostly, this whole configuration information about how an outbox should be rendered is provided via some options during setting outbox on an object.

Here is a simple API interface to demonstrate how an outbox is attached to a Schematic object and its configuration mechanism.

The add_outbox command allows user to add one or more outbox on objects.

add_outbox object_id -name n? ?-value value? ?-bgcolor n? ?-textcolor n? ?- -colorlist <string>?   ?-separatorcolor   n?   ?-crosscolor   n?   ?-deltaX   x?   \
            ?-deltaY y?

The object_id addresses the data base object, one of:inst, net, netBundle,port, portBus,pin,   pinBus,   hierPin   or   hierPinBus.
Please note:

Option **-bgcolor** <number> option specifies the color of outbox region. (default value is 1)
For ex : -bgcolor 2 specifies that the color of outbox region will be taken from the property   outboxcolor2.

Option **-textcolor** <number> option specifies the color of text for that particular outbox.
(default   value   is   0)
For ex : -textcolor 1 specifies that the color of text for outbox will be taken from the property   outboxcolor1.

Option **-crosscolor** <number> option specifies the color of cross for that particular outbox.   (default   value   is   4)
For ex : -crosscolor 1 specifies that the color of cross for outbox will be taken from the property   outboxcolor1.

Option **-colorlist** <string> option specifies the in order list of colors of regions for that particular   outbox.   (by   default   colorlist   is   empty   string)
For ex : -colorlist "3 5 4" specifies that the color of the first region of the outbox will be taken from the property outboxcolor3, color of second region from property outboxcolor5 and color of third region from property outboxcolor4.

Option **-deltaX** <number> specifies the horizontal shift.

Option **-deltaY** <number> specifies the vertical shift.

The text displayed in the callout box guides the user to resolve the problematic area of EDA design.

2.2. Algorithm for schematic view with callout box

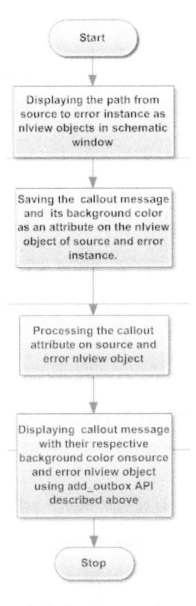

The following pseudo code depicts the example usage of Nlview TCL API for displaying the instances in schematic window with callout box.

proc analyzeDrc { } {

- *Add objects to schematic window*

- *Add callout specific attributes to same objects*

- *Display the objects and its associated attributes in the schematic window.*

}

3. Section2 : Enhance TCL/TK dialogue box

There is an enhanced TCL/TK dialogue box that is used to modify the background color of the text displayed in the callout box. The user can add/delete the text from the callout box using this dialogue box. The dialog box and mainly consist of a combo box, two list boxes, an option menu and Add/Remove button.

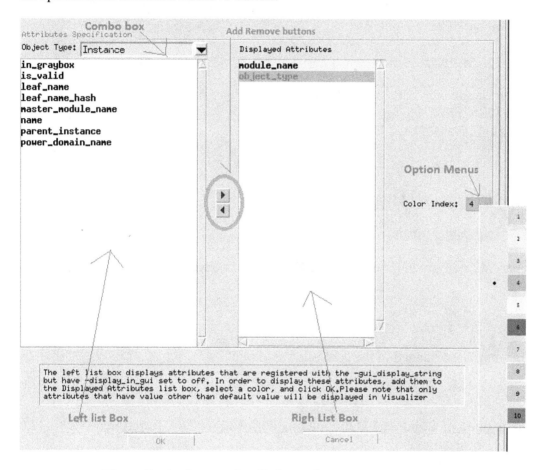

Figure2: An innovative dialogue box

3.1. Creation of Enhanced Dialogue box

The dialog box is also enhanced and mainly consists of a Combo-box, two list boxes, an option menu and Add/Remove buttons.

3.1.1. Combo box

The combo-box box is constructed using IWidgets combo-box .The user can select the category from Instances/Pins/Nets by using combo box and the respective attributes gets displayed in left /right list box.

3.1.2. Two list boxes

The two list boxes are scrolled list boxes and are constructed using list box and scroll bar of Tk widget.

3.1.3. Option menu

The Option menu is constructed using tk_Option Menu.

3.1.4. Text Message

The text message area is constructed using text widget of TK.

3.1.5. Add/Remove button

3.1.6. OK/Cancel button

The Add/Remove OK and Cancel buttons are constructed using button widgets of TK.

All the items are arranged in the grid using grid of TK.

3.2. Integration of Enhanced Dialogue box with Callout box functionality.

The user can select the category from Instances/Pins/Nets by using combo box and the respective attributes gets displayed in left /right list box. The attributes which are displayed in right list box gets displayed in callout box. The remaining attributes, displayed in the left list box are associated with the object type but are not displayed in the callout box .The user can add/remove attributes from left/right list using Add/Remove buttons. The respective changes will get applied to the callout box. The user can also modify the background color of the text displayed in the callout box by selecting a color in the option menu. These changes will also get applied to the callout box displayed in the schematic window.

3.3. Pseudo code for Integration of Dialogue Box with Callout Box

proc modifyCalloutBoxMessage { } {

1. *Creating individual widgets like combo box, scrolled listboxes and buttons and arranging them in grid.*

2. *The user can select an item from Pin/Instances/Nets from Combo-box , and the attributes of the same will be displayed in left and right list box*

3. *The user can also modify the background color of the attribute by selecting the appropriate color from the tk_option menu*

    OR

    The user can add/delete the attributes from left to right list box to display/remove the attributes from callout box.

    OR

    The user can execute both the steps.

4. *When the user press Ok button , these changes will be reflected in the callout box*

}

4. Glossary

GUI: Graphical User Interface.

HDL: Hardware description language.

DRC: Design Rule Checks.

5. Summary

Thus we display the DRC error information to user in an intuitive way. We can also modify the background color of the callout box using enhanced TCL/Tk dialogue. Thus we provide a guided debugging environment to the user by implementing and using the enhanced TCL/Tk widgets.

6. Bibliography

TCL wiki, http://wiki.tcl.tk

An Efficient Method for Rendering Design Schematics Using Tcl/Tk, and Distributed Relational Databases.

Manu Goel(manu_goel@mentor.com), Antara Ghosh(Antara_ghosh@mentor.com)
Mentor Graphics Corporation

Abstract:

Debugging a design in EDA is always a challenging and time consuming process. Designers need to have access to an efficient tool which can provide them the design connectivity in a logical and efficient manner. This paper discusses various challenges faced while writing such a tool for debugging a design and how were they handled to provide a fast and efficient solution. Schematic browser is a Tcl/Tk based GUI application, which user can use interactively to debug and understand the design.

Glossary:

Description of terms used in the paper:

Schematic Browser – Widget to view/trace the RTL level connectivity of a signal in a design
Incremental Mode – Browse the connectivity incrementally based on need
Full View Mode – View the connectivity of a particular segment of design in one go
Waveform Viewer – Widget to view the signal waveforms

Introduction:

The widget being discussed here is the schematic widget, which is a part of GUI provided with a typical simulator. The GUI is used to run simulation, view waveforms and then debug user design in case of any issues, using Schematic window/Wave window. Typically, user needs to compile the design with flags to turn on debugging and then use the GUI to verify/debug the design.

Schematic browser shows a graphical representation of a user's design. The tool converts the RTL constructs of user design, to their equivalent graphical symbols and presents them. The tool should be easy to use interactively to debug or understand the design. Viewing the design graphically, results into much faster debugging and clear insight in the design, making it easy for the user to correlate quickly about how his chip is going to behave.

Schematic window has two modes –

1. Interactive Design Mode: The purpose of this mode is to debug the design incrementally. For example, if the user finds any mismatch in his design output, they will start tracing the design in schematic window starting with the first signal which shows mismatch. User can then select any net and can choose to see the drivers or readers of the selected net to see the connectivity between various constructs around the net of interest. This mechanism can help him in identifying any misconnection or any unconnected logic.

2. Full Design mode: This mode is used to create full understanding of the design and it shows one full module at a time. This mode provides a compact view initially. User can expand to see more details on their area of interest and can compact that again whenever needed.

3. Batch Mode: There is a mode in this tool, where user can use the tool even without bringing up the GUI. This is called batch mode. In this mode, user gets an interactive prompt at the terminal itself, where user can perform certain operations. User can still use some of the above mentioned features in this mode. For example, they can request certain details through command and the details will be provided in text format.
Even when the GUI is up, user still has access to the prompt, and from there as well user can perform certain operations without actually opening up the Schematic browser GUI.

The GUI and the Schematic widget in discussion here are based on Tcl/Tk and the debug information is stored in a database software tool. User has the flexibility to open multiple instances of the Schematic browser and can perform independent operations in all of them in parallel.

Problem Statement:

As discussed, schematic viewer should be a intuitive tool for debugging any design. The Schematic viewer must give absolute clarity and maximum insight in the design to user, in real time. However, when the design is big, so is the netlist debug database. To manage such huge amount of data, fetch relevant information and drawing it in real time is a daunting task. To achieve that one must make sure there is as little as possible database interaction. That is, same query should not go to the database again and again.

So in one hand, the data access should be managed in a way, so that user can open debug netlist in multiple windows separately. These windows should be completely modular in behavior. Any change in one window, should not affect other windows in any manner. Consider a typical schematic rendering flow. Whenever logic is drawn in schematic window, there are safeguards to avoid painting same logic again. The scenario of repeated rendering can occur in two cases. One case is, the design has some looped logic, and while path browsing and incrementally drawing, the tool might go through same logic repeatedly. Second case is, the user has issued command to draw same logic more than once. To avoid these, there should be information present against every window, about what logic is already present in Schematic window. These caches of information is checked before drawing any logic, so that for an already drawn logic, the whole process of data fetching, processing and drawing is not repeated. Every netlist object must be processed (processing being the cycle from data fetching to netlist rendering) only once. However the tool must make sure, if the same net is drawn in different schematic window, which should be allowed. This is needed to maintain the window functional modularity as mentioned above.

On the other hand the tool needs to keep database interaction minimum. For example, as mentioned above, same logic should not be drawn in single Schematic window more than once, but same logic can be drawn in different schematic window. However, the effort of information fetching and processing should not be repeated for same logic. This is cardinal as, multiple accesses to debug database is costly and should be strictly guarded against.

The solution for this is to keep the data pool common among different Schematic window. Database access and initial data processing, which is same for all logic, regardless of which schematic window needs the information, should be done in a way so that the effort is not repeated. This is a must for good performance.

So the system has two apparently clashing goals. One is to keep the data model as mutually exclusive as possible to have correct functionality of multiple schematic viewers. The other is to have a common data pool and data processing algorithm.

Added to this is, another use of the system is working of Batch mode. As discussed in the introduction, this mode does not need any GUI window, so the system of information caching needed for schematic windows are not needed here. However this mode can also use the common data pool.

Lastly one must understand, as design gets bigger, DB size also gets bigger impacting the performance in multiple ways –
-   Loading the whole DB may take a lot of time
-   If full DB is loaded in memory, then memory footprint will increase causing the system to slow down.
-   Fetching the required information will be slower

So handling of database also have to be clever. Creating a monolithic database for whole design, and loading the whole database in memory, irrespective of user debug interest locality is wasteful and will harm netlist drawer's performance.

So to sum up, for schematic to be truly useful, it must have correct functionality, it must be reentrant and fast. The performance (time and memory) is almost as important as functionality is, for schematic debugging.

Solution

In order to create such a tool, the basic requirements are
- Tool should support multiple windows, which can provide similar functionality, but should be completely independent
- It should provide a clear interface to database from where all the necessary information can be fetched
- Whatever information is once processed should not be processed again.
- Non-GUI mode should also work

In order to provide the above functionality, advantage of **object oriented Tcl/Tk** is taken to create the main Schematic window widget. All common functionality that has to be provided and needed to be localized to a single window can be encapsulated inside a class. This class should have functionality of both, incremental and full view mode. Information, once loaded in a window needs to be cached, so that it can be brought back very quickly if user performs the same operation in that particular window. Such information is dependent on context of the window. So a localized caching is a must for such operations. This caching data structure, resides in the class created for the window. The class will also store all the user specified preferences for that particular window.

Second part of the problem is, to fetch the necessary information from the database to show the required functionality in GUI windows, as well as in non-GUI mode. Since a lot of information may be shared among various windows, keeping the code to fetch and store the information separate is a good idea. Since this information may be needed for non-GUI mode as well, it has to be outside the scope of main class creating the widget. Apart from this, since the design connectivity information will be same irrespective of the window from where the information is being requested, all information fetched for this is cached and can cater to future requests without having to go to debug database. So **Namespace** feature of Tcl/Tk came very handy here.

All interface APIs were protected inside the name space. The caching arrays were also protected inside the name space avoiding any misuse of these caches. Further, keeping these interfaces and caching outside the main class also helps batch mode, because that is not associated to any window, so the tool does not need to create any window object for non-GUI mode. It can simply work through fetching the information directly from these name space APIs.

Since the tool uses a lot of caching and the advantage of cache can be fully achieved only if the cached information can be fetched real quickly. The **associative arrays** of

Tcl were of great help for such a purpose. The logic of interest automatically became the key for such an array to store the information in the cache, and to fetch. One simply needs to check if such an entry exists in the concerned cache or not, and if it exists then the information is available very quickly. It does not require any hashing function implementation to store or retrieve the information form cache.

The information to be cached in these arrays is of the form of

```
Readers_of_net(/top/mid/in1) {/top/mid/o1 /top/mid/o2…}
```

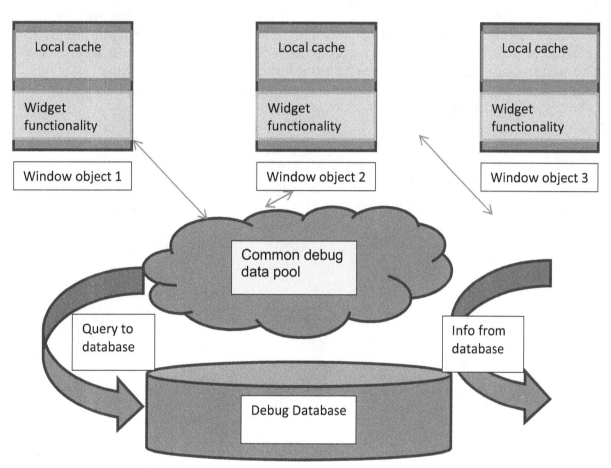

Figure 1: Window widget and debug data pool database

This is how the GUI side problem was solved, now comes the problem of managing the big database. Once that problem is solved, one can achieve a real efficient functionality that is needed. For this, again, Tcl came in very handy. The handling of a big database is divided into two parts. One, database should be modeled in such a way that data can be accessed efficiently. Two the data already fetched into memory should be cached and shared in judicious way among the different processes can access it independently.

The usual size of designs that simulator handle is hundreds of million gates. The debug database size can easily run into several hundred gigabytes. To keep a single monolithic database of that size and fetching information from it is time consuming. So instead of keeping single large design database, GUI should have several small databases for different parts of design.

Dividing databases into several parts also gives GUI the flexibility of generating different amount of debug information for different parts of the design, depending on the user's requirement. The simulator tool's debug database is arranged in a way that the tool maintains several databases for different parts of the design. These databases may have different amount of granularity of information on the parts of design it represents. This depth of the information for each part is dictated by the user. There is always one top node database that does the book keeping for the whole design. It would keep record of what part of design resides in which database. Also it keeps all the global information of the database.

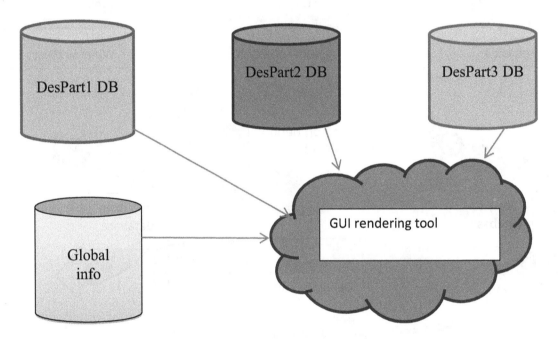

Figure 2: Debug database structure

The above picture shows flow of handling debug database by GUI rendering tool. The design is partitioned into Despart1, Despart2 and Despart3. The segregated parts of design produces separate debug databases. Different colors on the databases indicate that the debug data dumped for that part of the design are different. User has flexibility to modulate amount of database that will be dumped for different parts of design. This is the structure of database that the tool needs to handle.

Any standard database tool allows the user to access multiple databases through the handles they supply to user. The user must request the database tool to open a particular database (say db1) for information access; the tool does that and returns a handle (db1_handle). The user then must interact (execute queries to fetch relevant information) with the database (db1) through this handle (db1_handle).

The database structure for debugging as described above will have several databases and thus database handles for each. The top (or global) database will supply the databases with the path to each of these databases; however GUI must handle opening, accessing right database and closing them on its own. For this purpose the associative array of Tcl language comes in very handy once again. One can easily create an associative array for database handles. For example, for the above case discussed, the Tcl storage would be –

```
array set db_handle_array {}
set db_handle_array(db1)  db1_handle
```

Now, one can simply find out which queries should be carried out on which database (say db1) through the global database, and execute the queries on the database handle ($db_handle_array(db1) stored in the associative array. Because the array is associative, the worst time complexity to pick the correct handle is constant.

The second requirement of having a multiple database in a flexible GUI tool is, one opens a database only when that part of the design is accessed. So the database handles are created on the fly while drawing the part of the design that database holds. This again needs to be a fast (preferably in constant time) action for GUI. The GUI must in constant time determine if a database is already opened and handle is available if not then create that handle. Tcl gives a solution through where one can check if there is any value stored in an associative array against a particular key. So the algorithm of handling this flow would be -

```
If { [info exists db_handle_array(db1)] } {
    Use existing db handle
} else {
    Open db handle for db1
    Set db_handle_array(db1) db1_handle
}
```

The last requirement of handling multiple databases is, one must close all these handles before exiting GUI. Any database on which handle is kept open, might not behave correctly if a subsequent process tries to access it. However the flexibility that Tcl offers while accessing associative array fixes this problem. One can easily traverse an associative array like a list. The "array names" functionality brings all the keys of an associative array for the database handle arrays. The flow of closing all databases is –

```
foreach key [array names db_handle_array] {
    Close database whose handle is stored in
$db_handle_array($key)
}
```

Conclusion:

Using the above described approaches made as develop an efficient schematic widget
tool. IncrTcl helped us in creating the main window providing the needed functionality
and storing window specific information locally. Name spaced helped us in providing
well defined interface to fetch the required data and to manage a common cache of
data. This also helped in keeping the GUI side clean and clear from code to interact with
database and keeping the GUI code thin. Associative arrays helped significantly in
managing multiple databases parallel and at also helped in caching and retrieving the
data quickly and easily.
When all of these constructs of Tcl gets combined, then comes the real power of Tcl
through which, however complex the widget is, looks easy and trivial to create and
maintain.

Bibliography:

[1] An Object Oriented Mega-Widget Set, Mark L. Ulferts,
http://incrtcl.sourceforge.net/iwidgets/paper/paper.html

[2] TCL wiki, http://wiki.tcl.tk

[3] Can Distributed DB Provide An Effective Means Of Speeding Web Access Times,
Christopher G. Brown, http://jitm.ubalt.edu/XVIII-1/article1.pdf

[4] Using [incr Tcl] to improve stability of a GUI – A Case Study
http://www.tclcommunityassociation.org/wub/proceedings/Proceedings-
2009/proceedings/guis/incrtcl-emulation-debug-gui.pdf

www.ingramcontent.com/pod-product-compliance
Lightning Source LLC
Chambersburg PA
CBHW080415060326
40689CB00019B/4252